THE WOUNDED CHILD & THE NARCISSISTIC ADULT

HEALING IDENTITY FROM THE ROOTS

WRITTEN BY

Edna L. Isaac

JDN Publications

WWW.JDNPUBLICATIONS.COM

The Wounded Child and the Narcissistic Adult

Healing Identity From the Roots

ISBN: 978-1-938432-64-4 (Paperback)

ISBN: 978-1-938432-65-1 (Ebook)

Copyright © 2026 by Edna L. Isaac

All rights reserved. No part of this book may be reproduced, stored, or transmitted in any form or by any means—electronic, mechanical, photocopying, recording, or otherwise—without prior written permission from the publisher or the author, except as permitted under United States copyright law.

Disclaimer

JDN/EDUCATE Publishing is a self-publishing platform that allows authors to publish their works without undergoing an editorial selection process.

Authors are solely responsible for the content of their works. JDN/EDUCATE does not necessarily share or endorse the opinions expressed in this book. We are not responsible for errors, omissions, or consequences arising from its use. Readers should be aware that the content of this book is the sole responsibility of the author.

This book was written and designed with the assistance of AI.

Printed in the United States of America

TABLE OF CONTENTS

PROLOGUE *The Wounded Child And The Narcissistic Adult*	1
INTRODUCTION *We All Carry a Story*	3
CHAPTER 1 *The Child Who Learned To Survive*	7
CHAPTER 2 *When The Heart Hardens To Avoid Feeling*	23
CHAPTER 3 *Narcissism As A Defense Mechanism*	31
CHAPTER 4 *Marriages Affected By Childhood Trauma*	41
CHAPTER 5 *Wounded Leaders Who Wound*	49
CHAPTER 6 *The Spiritual Cost Of Unhealed Trauma*	55
CHAPTER 7 *The Encounter With Christ The Healer*	65
CHAPTER 8 *Healing The Inner Child*	75
CHAPTER 9 *Relearning To Love Without Fear*	83
CHAPTER 10 *Restored Relationships*	93
CHAPTER 11 *A New Identity in Christ*	103
CONCLUSION *The Story Does Not End At The Wound*	113
EPILOGUE *The Beauty Of What God Restores*	121
30-DAY EMOTIONAL HEALING PLAN *A Daily Journey Toward Restoration*	125

STUDY GUIDE FOR GROUPS AND LEADERS	141
ABOUT THE AUTHOR	159
REFERENCES	163

PROLOGUE

THE WOUNDED CHILD AND THE NARCISSISTIC ADULT

Some stories begin long before we are able to remember them. Stories written in silence, in glances, in absences, in words never spoken, and in wounds no one knew how to name. This book is born precisely from that place: from the inner child who was once wounded, and from the adult who, without realizing it, learned to survive from that wound.

Throughout my journey as a counselor, pastor, educator, and as a woman who has also had to face her own shadows, I have seen how many adults live trapped in patterns they do not understand. They react harshly, manipulate unintentionally, withdraw, hurt others, or hide behind masks... unaware that, deep within, there is a child crying out to be seen, heard, and healed.

This book does not seek to assign blame or justify harmful behaviors. It seeks to understand. It seeks to illuminate. It seeks to heal. Because behind every narcissistic adult—whether mild, moderate, or severe—there is often a child who learned to protect themselves in ways that have now become destructive.

My intention is to take you by the hand through an honest, compassionate, and revealing journey. A journey where you will be able to recognize your own wounds, understand the emotional dynamics that have shaped you, and discover that healing is not only possible but necessary to break cycles and reclaim your true identity.

This book is not a judgment. It is a mirror.
It is not a condemnation. It is an invitation.
It is not a story of pain. It is a story of restoration.

My prayer is that as you read these pages, the Holy Spirit will lovingly reveal what still needs to be embraced, forgiven, and transformed. That you may look at your inner child with tenderness and at your adult self with hope. And that you may discover that God has never left you alone in your process; He has been with you from the very beginning, waiting for the moment you dare to heal.

Welcome to this journey.
Welcome to your truth.
Welcome to your restoration.

INTRODUCTION
WE ALL CARRY A STORY

Over the past few months, before God gifted me this book, I have been living an experience that has marked my life. I have had the opportunity to live with my father, with whom I had not lived since I was nine years old. Today, he is an 80-year-old man, in a stage of life where many had already counted him out. This time together was not a coincidence; it was the answer to a prayer I made from the deepest part of my heart. At that time, he was in a place where all that was expected was his death, a hospice nursing home. I asked God to allow me to bring him home, give him a dignified room, and ensure that his final days would be lived with respect, care, and a measure of the dignity that life had taken from him.

His situation was painful. According to him, his wife of more than forty years had left him there, with no plans to return. And it was true. While we were in Puerto Rico searching for him, she neither called nor came by, even though she was only a few minutes away. That absence echoed many of the wounds he had carried in silence.

Today, my father is writing his own book: *Abandoned to Oblivion but Loved by God*, where he shares part of his story. And as we gathered his memories, God began to minister to me deeply. It was in that process that this book was born. Before it ever reached your hands, this message first touched my heart. Because even though we are Christians, even though we love God, we all have hidden corners in the soul where narcissism has shown its face. Sometimes we express it without realizing it. Sometimes we justify it. But many times, we simply do not know how to identify it, much less how to heal it.

This book is an invitation to look within. To recognize that although we love Christ and desire to do good, there are patterns that were formed in us since childhood—before we had words, before we understood what it meant to be loved or rejected.

Many of us grew up in homes where there was love, but also silence. Where there was provision, but not affection. Where there was expectation, but not validation. And others, unfortunately, grew up in homes marked by abuse, abandonment, or violence—as was my case, and my father's, and his father's before him.

Childhood leaves marks. Some are visible. Others are hidden in the deepest parts of the soul.

This book was born to illuminate those marks. To show how childhood trauma shapes our identity, our relationships, our spirituality, and the way we love. To reveal how a wounded child can become an adult who protects themselves with coldness, control, distance, or defensive narcissism.

But it was also born to bring hope. Because what was wounded can be healed. What was broken can be restored. What was distorted can be redeemed.

This book is not just information. It is a path. A process. An invitation to reconnect with your story, embrace your truth, heal your inner child, and discover your identity in Christ.

My prayer is that every page becomes a mirror, a hug, and a door.

A mirror to see your reality.
A hug to validate your pain.
A door into the freedom God has for you.

CHAPTER 1
THE CHILD WHO LEARNED TO SURVIVE

How Early Trauma Shapes Identity

As we have mentioned, each one of us carries within a story we did not choose. A story that began before we had words, before we could defend ourselves, before we understood what it meant to be loved or rejected. At some point in our childhood, we learned to survive. And that learning—although it saved us in that moment—became the emotional structure that now defines how we think, how we feel, how we love, and how we react.

This chapter is an invitation to look back, not to blame, but to understand. Because what is not understood is repeated. And what is repeated without awareness becomes a generational cycle.

1. THE ORIGIN OF THE WOUND: WHEN THE WORLD WAS TOO BIG

Childhood is sacred territory. It is the place where our identity is formed, where our capacity to trust develops, where our perception of love takes shape, and where we learn— or fail to learn—what it means to be seen, heard, and valued. But for many of us, that sacred territory became an emotional battlefield. According to Orth, Krauss, and Back (2024), narcissistic patterns can develop as an early response to emotional insecurity.

Some grew up in homes where there was love, yes... but also chaos, shouting, tension, and silences that hurt more than words. Others grew up in homes where there was provision but no affection; where there was food on the table but no hugs; where there was a roof but no emotional refuge. Others grew up in homes where there was expectation but no validation; where everything had to be done "right," yet it was never enough. And others, unfortunately, grew up in homes marked by abuse, abandonment, violence, or indifference.

Many of us grew up hearing phrases that pierced the soul:

- "You're good for nothing."
- "You're a burden."
- "You always do everything wrong."
- "You're just like your father."
- "Be quiet, no one wants to hear you."
- "Don't be weak."

Words that seemed like simple scoldings but became deep wounds. Words that shaped how we see ourselves and how we relate to others. Without realizing it, those voices began to direct our behavior: how we love, how we react, how we defend ourselves, how we hide.

But there is something fundamental we must understand. A child does not have the capacity to interpret what they live. A child cannot say:

- "My mother is emotionally absent because she is wounded too."
- "My father yells because he doesn't know how to manage his emotions."
- "My caregiver doesn't hug me because they never learned how to love."
- "My parents are repeating patterns they themselves suffered."

A child does not analyze. A child does not rationalize. A child does not understand the emotional complexity of adults.

A child only feels.

And what they feel—rejection, fear, abandonment, confusion, loneliness—becomes their absolute truth.

A child thinks:

- "If they yell at me, it's because I'm the problem."
- "If they don't hug me, it's because I don't deserve love."

- "If they ignore me, it's because I'm worthless."
- "If they compare me, it's because I'm not enough."

And that innocent yet devastating interpretation becomes the root of the emotional wound we carry into adulthood.

The wound is not born from the event... it is born from the child's interpretation.

Psychological literature shows that narcissism does not arise from grandiosity but from deep childhood wounds (Back & Morf, 2020).

And that interpretation—made with a small heart in a world far too big—is what defines how we learn to love, defend ourselves, relate, and survive.

2. The Brain in Survival Mode

When a child experiences trauma—whether big or small—their brain does something extraordinary: it reorganizes itself to protect them.

- Not to make them happy.
- Not to help them develop.
- But to keep them alive.
- This is not a conscious decision.
- It is not something the child chooses.
- It is an automatic, biological, instinctive mechanism.

Therefore, the child's brain learns to:

- Shut down emotions to avoid pain.
- Scan the environment to anticipate danger.
- Adapt to instability, even if it is unfair or harmful.
- Become a "little adult"—responsible, quiet, or compliant.
- Disconnect from the body because fear feels too overwhelming.

This process creates what we call **survival mode**.

Survival mode is not a feeling… it is an entire system.

It is not just being sad, scared, or confused. It is a state where the whole body and mind work to avoid further harm.

A child in survival mode learns to:

- Not cry, because crying brings punishment or ridicule.
- Not ask, because asking brings rejection.
- Not trust, because trusting has been dangerous.
- Not depend, because depending means being hurt.
- Not show vulnerability, because vulnerability was used against them.

This child learns to live on alert, tense, guarded. They learn to read faces, tones of voice, and silences. They learn to "behave," to not bother, to not take up space. But here is the most painful part…

. . .

That child grows.

- Their body grows.
- Their age changes.
- Their environment changes.

But their emotional system does not grow with them. The brain continues functioning as if the danger were real, even when it no longer is.

- It keeps shutting down emotions.
- It keeps distrusting.
- It keeps protecting itself.
- It keeps surviving... even as an adult.

The Adult Who Lives in Survival Mode

This adult may appear strong, independent, cold, or self-sufficient. But inside, they are still a child who learned to survive without support.

> It's not that they don't want to feel.
> Their brain learned not to.
> It's not that they don't want to trust.
> Their defense system won't allow it.
> It's not that they don't want to love.
> Love feels dangerous.
> This adult is not broken.
> Not beyond repair. Not condemned.
> They are programmed to survive.
> And now they are learning to live.

3. EMOTIONAL DISCONNECTION: THE FIRST DEFENSE

When the pain is too great, the child does not look for a strategy... they look to survive. And the fastest way to survive is not to understand, confront, or process. The fastest way is to disconnect. Not because they want to. Not because they are strong. Not because they are rebellious. But because they have no other option.

Emotional disconnection is anesthesia for the soul

Just as the body faints to avoid feeling a blow that is too strong, the child's heart "shuts down" to avoid feeling what is destroying them. Emotional disconnection is an emergency mechanism.

It is the child's way of saying:

"If I feel this, I won't be able to bear it."

So they learn to:

- Not cry
- Not ask
- Not need
- Not expect
- Not trust

They learn to live without feeling because feeling hurts too much.

How does this disconnection form?

It happens when the child experiences situations that exceed their emotional capacity:

- Constant yelling
- Humiliation
- Rejection
- Abandonment
- Physical or verbal violence
- Cold silences
- Disproportionate punishments
- Total lack of affection
- Or the constant feeling of walking "on tiptoe" to avoid upsetting someone

The child thinks:

> *"If I don't feel, it won't hurt."*
> *"If I don't need, they won't reject me."*
> *"If I don't speak, they won't yell at me."*
> *And little by little, they disconnect from themselves.*

The Adult Born From That Disconnection

That disconnected child grows and becomes an adult who:

- Doesn't know how to express emotions because it was never safe to do so.
- Doesn't know how to ask for help because they learned no one would come.
- Doesn't know how to identify what they feel because they shut down emotions to survive.

- Doesn't trust anyone because trusting was dangerous.
- Feels alone even when surrounded by people because disconnection became a habit.
- Protects themselves with coldness, control, or distance because it is the only way they know to avoid being hurt again.

> This adult is not cold.
> Not selfish.
> Not insensitive.
> **They are a survivor.**

Someone who learned to live without feeling because feeling, in childhood, was too dangerous. Emotional disconnection is not a defect... it is a wound. And like every wound, it can be healed. But first, it must be recognized. No one can reconnect with their emotions until they understand why they had to shut them down.

4. THE PRIMARY WOUND: "I AM NOT ENOUGH"

Every deep emotional wound has a root.

And that root almost always comes down to one phrase that brands the soul like hot iron:

"Something in me was not enough to be loved."

This is the lie that marks the story of millions of children. It does not come from truth but from the innocent interpretation of a heart that does not yet know how to defend itself. A child does not understand trauma, generational wounds, broken parents, or emotionally immature adults. A child only understands what they feel. And what they feel becomes identity.

When Words Become Scars

Imagine a girl who grows up hearing:

- "You're good for nothing."
- "You're useless."
- "You're a burden."
- "You don't do anything right."
- "You're lazy."
- "You're not even good enough to walk a dog."

Or a boy who, every time he tries to help, play, or express himself, hears:

- "Be quiet."
- "You always do it wrong."
- "You can't."
- "You don't learn."
- "You're worthless."

The child does not think:

- "My mother is wounded."
- "My father doesn't know how to love."
- "My caregivers lack emotional tools."

No.

The child thinks:

"I am the problem."

Thus, the absence of affection is interpreted as a personal defect.

- Abuse is interpreted as guilt.
- Abandonment is interpreted as a lack of worth.
- Expectation is interpreted as incapacity.

The Lie That Becomes Identity

What began as a hurtful phrase, a look of contempt, or a prolonged silence becomes an internal voice that follows them throughout life:

- "I'm not enough."
- "I don't deserve love."
- "I have to try harder."
- "If I fail, they'll reject me."
- "If I show my emotions, they'll hurt me."
- "If I'm not perfect, I'm worthless."

That voice becomes a defense system. A way to survive. A mask.

The Adult Born From a Wounded Child

The adult who emerges from that wound lives with a constant sense of:

- Insecurity, because they never learned to feel safe.
- Shame, because they believe something is wrong with them.
- Self-criticism, because they repeat the voices that Perfectionism, because they think only being flawless will make them acceptable.
- Need for approval, because their worth always depended on others.
- Fear of rejection, because rejection was their first emotional teacher.

And this primary wound—this lie planted in childhood—becomes the seed of:

> Defensive narcissism, emotional coldness, inability to trust, difficulty loving without fear, and the tendency to protect oneself even when there is no danger.

The Root of Narcissism Is Not Pride... It Is Pain

Many adults who seem cold, distant, arrogant, or controlling are actually wounded children who learned to survive without love. Children who grew up believing that feeling was dangerous. Children who promised themselves:

"I will never allow anyone to hurt me again."

And that promise, made from pain, becomes a wall.

5. STORIES THAT REPEAT: THE GENERATIONAL CYCLE

What is not healed is inherited. Not because we want to, but because we don't know how to do it differently.

A wounded child becomes an adult who:

- Loves with fear
- Parents with insecurity
- Leads with control
- Relates from defense
- Reacts from trauma

And without meaning to, they reproduce what they lived. But here is the good news:

The story can be rewritten.
Healing is possible.
Identity can be restored.
And the inner child can be embraced,
heard, and transformed.

PRACTICAL EXERCISE: EMOTIONAL TIMELINE

This exercise will help you see your story with greater clarity.

You don't need to be an expert—only honest with yourself.

1. **Draw a horizontal line**

   - On a sheet of paper, draw a straight line from left to right.

2. **Mark your birth and your current age**

   - On the left end, write: "Birth."
   - On the right end, write your current age.

This line represents your entire life.

3. **Mark the important moments that shaped you**

Along the line, place dots or short notes where you remember emotionally impactful moments, such as:

- Wounds (something that hurt you)
- Losses (people, places, stability)
- Major changes (moves, divorces, separations)
- Moments of fear
- Moments of loneliness or abandonment

You don't need to write much. A word or short phrase is enough.

Examples:

- "Dad's beatings"
- "Mom said I was worthless."
- "Left alone"
- "Called lazy"
- "Told I never did anything right"

4. Now mark the moments of love or support

In another color (if possible), add the moments when you did receive:

- Affection
- Protection
- Encouraging words
- Someone who cared for or defended you

This will help you see that your story has both light and shadow.

5. Observe your line

Look at it calmly. Ask yourself:

- Are there more moments of pain than love?
- Are there stages where you felt very alone?
- Are there patterns that repeat?
- Was there someone who marked you for better or worse?

6. Reflect with these questions

Write whatever comes out, without judging yourself:

- What did I learn to do in order to survive?
  - (Stay quiet, please others, hide my emotions, be strong, not ask for help...)
- What emotions did I stop feeling to protect myself?
  - (Sadness, fear, joy, vulnerability...)
- What parts of me remained trapped in childhood?
  - (My voice, my innocence, my trust, my ability to play, my sense of worth...)

Why is this exercise so important?

Because it allows you to see your life from above, as if observing it from God's perspective: with clarity, compassion, and purpose.

It helps you understand why you are the way you are, and where the wound began that you are now ready to heal.

Closing Prayer for the Chapter

Beloved God,

Show me through Your Holy Spirit the child I once was. Show me their wounds, their fears, their silences. Help me see them with compassion, not judgment. Teach me to embrace them as You embrace me. Heal me from the root. Make me free to love without fear.

In Jesus' name, Amen.

CHAPTER 2
WHEN THE HEART HARDENS TO AVOID FEELING

The Cost of Shutting Down Emotions

Some wounds do not bleed, but leave invisible scars. Some pains do not scream, but silence the soul. And some hearts are not broken outwards, but inwards.

When a child grows up in an environment where feeling is dangerous, expressing emotions is risky, or needing help is a source of shame, they learn to harden their heart. Not out of malice. Not out of rebellion. But for survival. Research indicates that the infant brain adapts to survive, even if that means temporarily suppressing essential emotions (Orth et al., 2024).

This chapter explores that silent, profound process— **how a tender heart becomes a hardened heart**, and how that hardening affects adult life, relationships, spirituality, and identity.

1. THE HEART THAT SHUTS DOWN TO SURVIVE

The human heart was designed to feel. To love, cry, laugh, connect, trust, express, and receive. But when the environment isn't safe, the heart learns to shut down.

A child who lives:

- Rejection
- Abandonment
- Constant criticism
- Emotional violence
- Indifference
- Extreme demand
- Instability
- lack of affection

Learn that feeling hurts. And that in order to survive, he must stop feeling. This emotional shutting down is not a conscious decision. It is an automatic mechanism of the soul. The child thinks, *"If I don't feel, it doesn't hurt." "If I don't need to, they don't reject me." "If I don't show, they don't hurt me."* And so the hardened heart is born.

2. EMOTIONAL ANESTHESIA: A REFUGE THAT BECOMES A PRISON

Emotional anesthesia is like a cold blanket covering the heart. It protects, but it also isolates. It avoids pain, but it also prevents love.

. . .

The anesthetized child becomes an adult who:

- Doesn't know what he feels
- Cannot express emotions
- Disconnects in times of conflict
- Avoid deep conversations
- Is uncomfortable with vulnerability
- It is protected with silence, distance, or coldness
- Confuses calm with disconnection
- Confuses control with strength

What began as a refuge becomes a prison. The person does not suffer "too much." He suffers "less". Not because there is no pain, but because he cannot access it.

3. THE FUNCTIONAL BUT EMOTIONALLY DISCONNECTED ADULT

Many adults who grew up with early trauma are highly functional. They work, lead, serve, produce, help, and solve. From the outside, they seem strong, stable, capable. Emotional disconnection is a common response in children exposed to unpredictable or emotionally insecure environments (Yakeley, 2018).

This emotional disconnection drags them into their adult life, but inside, they live disconnected. They are people who:

- Feel that "something is missing."
- Fail to fully enjoy
- Live in autopilot status

- Feel lonely even when accompanied
- They don't know how to get love
- Are uncomfortable with emotional intimacy
- Avoid conflict or face it harshly
- Feel "empty" without knowing why

Emotional disconnection is not a lack of love. It is lack of access to love.

4. THE BODY AS AN ARCHIVE OF UNPROCESSED PAIN

When the heart hardens, the body becomes the archive of pain.

The body keeps:

- Tensions
- Chronic pain
- Anxiety
- Insomnia
- Emotional fatigue
- Overreactions
- Hypervigilance
- Digestive problems
- Shallow breathing

The body speaks what the heart is silent.

Many adults say, *"I don't know why I react like that." "I don't know why I feel so tense." "I don't know why I have such a hard* time trusting." "I don't know why I shut down when someone approaches."

The answer lies in childhood. In the heart that learned to harden itself to survive.

5. THE INABILITY TO ASK FOR HELP: THE DEEPEST WOUND

A child who did not receive help when he needed it learns not to ask for it. Learn that dependence is dangerous. That needing is embarrassing. That showing weakness is risky. That child becomes an adult who:

- Doesn't ask for support
- Does not express needs
- Shows no vulnerability
- Feels uncomfortable receiving love
- Feels guilty when you need something
- It is required to be strong all the time

The inner phrase is, "If I ask, I'm rejected." "If I show, they hurt me." "If I need to, they abandon me."

That's why many hardened adults seem self-sufficient. But they are not. They are only protected.

6. THE HARDENED HEART IN RELATIONSHIPS

Emotional hardening profoundly affects relationships; for instance, we can see it in different relationships:

. . .

In marriage

- Emotional intimacy is avoided
- You respond with coldness or silence
- Distance is confused with peace
- The vulnerability of the other is interpreted as a threat
- Reacts with defense instead of connection

In the family

- He loves himself, but without expressing it
- Provided, but not connected
- You are present, but emotionally absent

In the church or community

- It is served without allowing itself to be served
- He leads without allowing himself to be accompanied
- He helps himself without allowing himself to be helped
- The hardened heart can love, but it cannot feel loved.

7. THE SPIRITUAL COST OF A HARDENED HEART

Emotional disconnection also affects spiritual life.

Just to name a few of the areas in your spiritual life that can be affected, a hardened heart:

- **Prayer:** Prays, but does not feel.
- **Service:** Serves, but is not surrendered.
- **Worship:** Worships, but does not yield.
- **Sensitivity:** Listens, but does not receive.
- **Trusting:** Believes, but does not trust.

Not because he doesn't love God, but because he doesn't know how to open up. The relationship with God becomes intellectual, not intimate. Functional, not emotional. Correct, but not profound. God wants to touch areas the person has learned to protect — and that produces resistance.

8. THE PROCESS OF SOFTENING THE HEART

The hardened heart does not soften strongly. It is not softened by guilt. It does not soften with demand. Softens with:

- Security
- Patience
- Constant love
- Gradual vulnerability
- Safe spaces
- Divine Presence
- Emotional accompaniment
- Truth without judgment

The hardened heart does not need pressure. It needs permission. Permission to feel. Permission to cry. Permission to need. Permission to be human.

PRACTICAL EXERCISE: IDENTIFYING MY EMOTIONAL DEFENSES

Answer honestly:

1. What emotions do I avoid feeling?
2. What situations make me disconnect?
3. What do I do when someone gets emotionally close to me?
4. What did I learn in my childhood about expressing emotions?
5. What part of me am I protecting when I shut down?

Then write a phrase of compassion toward yourself: "I'm learning to feel again. I'm safe."

Chapter Closing Prayer

Lord, show me the areas where my heart has become hardened. Not to judge me, but to heal me. Teach me to feel without fear, to open up without shame, to trust without running away. Soften my heart with your love. Make me sensitive to your voice, your presence, and the people you have placed in my life. Amen.

CHAPTER 3
NARCISSISM AS A DEFENSE MECHANISM

It's Not Ego... It's Fear

The word *"narcissism"* is often used as a moral judgment. It is associated with selfishness, arrogance, coldness, manipulation, or lack of empathy. But behind many narcissistic behaviors, there is no malice—there is unhealed pain. There is no pride—there is deep shame. There is no self-sufficiency—there is fear of abandonment. This chapter does not seek to justify harmful behaviors, but to understand their root. Because what is understood can be transformed. And what is transformed stops causing harm.

1. NARCISSISM AS EMOTIONAL ARMOR

Narcissism is not born in adulthood. It does not appear suddenly. It is not a trait someone chooses. Narcissism is an emotional armor formed in childhood when a child learns that:

- Showing vulnerability is dangerous
- Depending on others is risky
- Expressing emotions is useless
- Asking for affection leads to rejection
- Being authentic brings shame

The wounded child creates an *"alternate self,"* an inflated version of themselves that protects them from pain. That *alternate self* is what we call the **false self**.

2. THE FALSE SELF: THE MASK THAT PROTECTS THE INNER CHILD

The false self is an emotional construction designed for survival. It is the mask that says:

- "I'm fine."
- "I don't need anyone."
- "I can do it alone."
- "It doesn't affect me."
- "I don't care."

But behind that mask is a child thinking:

- "If I show my need, I'll be rejected."
- "If I show my pain, I'll be humiliated."
- "If I show my fragility, I'll be destroyed."

The false self is not arrogance. It is protection.

3. VULNERABLE NARCISSISM VS. GRANDIOSE NARCISSISM

There are two primary expressions of defensive narcissism:

1. **Vulnerable Narcissism**

(the most common in wounded individuals)

- Hypersensitivity
- Fear of rejection
- Need for approval
- Deep insecurity
- Constant shame
- Emotional withdrawal
- Victimization
- Difficulty receiving correction

This form of narcissism does not look like arrogance—it looks like protected fragility.

2. GRANDIOSE NARCISSISM

(the most visible mask)

- Control
- Perfectionism
- Need to be right
- Difficulty apologizing
- Apparent superiority
- Emotional coldness
- Demanding attitudes

- Inability to acknowledge mistakes

This form of narcissism is not a strength. It is fear disguised as power. Both are born from the same place: an unattended childhood wound.

4. TOXIC SHAME: THE HIDDEN ROOT

Toxic shame is the deep belief that *"there is something wrong with me."*

It is not guilt for what I did. It is a shame for who I am.

A child who grows up with toxic shame thinks:

- "I'm not enough."
- "I'm not worthy of love."
- "I have no value."
- "I'm a problem."
- "I'm too much."
- "I'm not enough."

To survive that shame, the child creates a defensive identity —one that says:

- "I am special."
- "I am strong."
- "I don't need anyone."
- "I am in control."

But that identity is not real. It is armor.

5. THE NEED TO BE SERVED: A CRY FROM THE INNER CHILD

The narcissistic adult demands what they never received:

- Attention
- Validation
- Recognition
- Affirmation
- Care
- Priority

They do not ask with words. They demand with attitudes. Not because they are selfish, but because their inner child is still hungry. Narcissism is a desperate attempt to fill an emotional void formed in childhood.

6. THE INABILITY TO RECIPROCATE: WHEN THE HEART NEVER LEARNED TO LOVE

Defensive narcissism does not know how to love maturely. Not because it doesn't want to, but because it never learned how. The wounded child did not receive:

- Empathy
- Attentive listening
- Validation
- Secure affection
- Healthy boundaries
- Emotional presence

Therefore, the adult cannot give what they never received. Narcissism is not lack of love. It is lack of tools.

7. FEAR OF VULNERABILITY: THE ROOT OF HARDNESS

Vulnerability is the greatest enemy of narcissism—because vulnerability exposes the inner child.

The narcissistic adult fears:

- Being seen
- Being known
- Being corrected
- Being rejected
- Being abandoned
- Being insufficient

So they protect themselves with:

- Control
- Distance
- Criticism
- Perfectionism
- Silence
- Superiority

It is not pride. It is fear.

8. NARCISSISM IN RELATIONSHIPS: A PAINFUL CYCLE

Defensive narcissism creates unbalanced relationships.

In Marriage

- One gives more
- The other demands more
- One seeks connection
- The other seeks control
- One wants to talk
- The other shuts down

In the Family

- Love exists, but without empathy
- Provision exists, but without a connection
- Correction exists, but without tenderness

In Church or Leadership

- Leadership from insecurity
- Authority is confused with control
- Obedience demanded without relationship
- Spiritual vulnerability avoided

Narcissism does not destroy out of malice. It destroys out of fear.

9. THE POSSIBILITY OF TRANSFORMATION

The good news is this: **defensive narcissism can be healed.**

Because it is not an identity, it is a defense.

And every defense can be dismantled when there is:

- Safety
- Consistent love
- Healthy boundaries
- Emotional support
- Compassionate confrontation
- God's presence
- Therapeutic processes
- Gradual vulnerability

Narcissism is not broken by force. It melts with love.

PRACTICAL EXERCISE: IDENTIFYING MY MASKS

Answer honestly:

1. What parts of myself do I show to appear strong?
2. What parts of myself do I hide out of fear of being hurt?
3. What do I need but don't know how to ask for?
4. What am I afraid to reveal?
5. What mask do I use when I feel insecure?

Then write this declaration:

"My worth is not in my mask. My worth is in who God says I am."

Closing Prayer

Lord, show me the masks I have used to survive—not to shame me, but to set me free. Heal me from the shame that made me hide. Teach me to live from my true self, the one You created, the one You love, the one that needs no masks to be accepted. Make me free to love and to be loved. Amen.

CHAPTER 4

MARRIAGES AFFECTED BY CHILDHOOD TRAUMA

When Two Wounded Children Try to Love as Adults

Marriage is one of the places where childhood trauma manifests most intensely. Not because the spouse is the problem, but because intimacy reveals what distance hides. Recent studies confirm that the lack of emotional validation in childhood contributes to the development of narcissistic defenses in adulthood (EBSCO Research Starters, n.d.). In daily life, in emotional closeness, in the vulnerability that love requires, once dormant wounds begin to surface. Marriage becomes a mirror that reflects not only who we are today, but who we were yesterday. This chapter explores how two incomplete emotional stories can collide, how childhood trauma affects communication, intimacy, and connection, and how healing becomes possible when both partners choose to walk toward truth with humility and compassion.

1. MARRIAGE: THE STAGE WHERE THE INNER CHILD AWAKENS

Marriage does not unite only two adults. It unites two stories, two childhoods, two wounds, and two survival strategies.

This is why, when a couple faces repetitive conflicts, they are not always arguing about what they think they are. Many times, they are arguing from their inner child.

Common examples:

- The one who fears abandonment clings.
- The one who fears intrusion withdraws.
- The one who learned to stay silent disconnects.
- The one who learned to defend themselves attacks.
- The one who was never heard raises their voice.
- The one who was never validated demands.

It is not two adults fighting. It is two wounded children reacting.

2. INTIMACY AS A TRAUMA TRIGGER

Emotional intimacy is beautiful, but it is also dangerous for someone who grew up without emotional safety.

Intimacy activates:

- fear of rejection
- fear of being seen

- fear of being insufficient
- fear of losing control
- fear of depending
- fear of being hurt

This is why many people who long for love also avoid it. They want closeness, but they fear the vulnerability that closeness requires.

Marriage becomes a battlefield between the desire to connect and the fear of being hurt.

3. THE CONFLICT CYCLE: WHEN THE WOUND LEADS THE CONVERSATION

Most marital conflicts do not begin with a real problem, but with an unattended emotion.

Example of the cycle:

1. One feels ignored.
2. The other feels attacked.
3. One demands.
4. The other defends.
5. One cries.
6. The other shuts down.
7. Both feel misunderstood.

And the cycle repeats.

They are not fighting about the trash, the money, the schedule, or the routine. They are fighting for:

- feeling seen
- feeling loved
- feeling safe
- feeling important

The conflict is the symptom. The wound is the root.

4. FEAR OF VULNERABILITY: THE ENEMY OF LOVE

Love requires vulnerability. But trauma teaches self-protection.

This is why, in many marriages:

- One wants to talk
- The other wants to avoid
- One wants closeness
- The other wants space
- One wants resolution
- The other wants silence

Each believes the other is the problem. But the true enemy is fear.

- Fear of being seen.
- Fear of being rejected.
- Fear of not being enough.
- Fear of repeating the story.

5. IMPOSSIBLE COMMUNICATION: WHEN THE HEART IS IN DEFENSE MODE

When trauma is activated, communication becomes distorted.

- The one who feels abandoned says, "**Why aren't you here?**"
    - But what they mean is: "**Am I important to you?**"
- The one who feels invaded says, "**Leave me alone.**"
    - But what they mean is: "**I need space to feel safe.**"
- The one who feels criticized says, "**You're always attacking me.**"
    - But what they mean is: "**It hurts to feel like I'm not enough.**"
- The one who feels ignored says, "**You never listen to me.**"
    - But what they mean is: "**I need to know my voice matters.**"

Communication becomes impossible when each person speaks from their wound instead of their heart.

6. MARRIAGE AS A PLACE OF HEALING

Although marriage can activate wounds, it can also heal them. Not because the spouse is responsible for curing the other, but because secure love creates an environment where healing becomes possible.

Healing occurs when:

- Listening happens without judgment
- Validation happens without minimizing
- Love is given without conditions
- Healthy boundaries are established
- Empathy is practiced
- Each partner acknowledges the other's story
- Forgiveness is learned and received

Marriage does not heal by magic. It heals by presence.

7. TOOLS FOR MARRIAGES IMPACTED BY CHILDHOOD TRAUMA

1. Safe Communication

- Speak from "I feel," not "You always."
- Pause when trauma is activated.
- Name emotions before discussing issues.

2. Gradual Vulnerability

- Share small fears first.
- Practice emotional honesty without pressure.

3. Emotional Validation

- "I understand why you feel that way."
- "Your emotion is valid."
- "I'm here with you."

4. Healthy Boundaries

- Space when needed.
- Closeness when safe.

5. Recognizing Patterns

- What triggers my wound?
- What triggers my partner's?

6. Replacing Reactions with Responses

- Breathe
- Pause
- Name
- Choose

A healthy marriage is not perfect. It is aware.

PRACTICAL EXERCISE: "WHAT I FEEL VS. WHAT I SAY"

Complete these sentences:

1. When I say "leave me," what I really feel is…
2. When I say "you don't listen," what I really need is…
3. When I get angry, what I'm really afraid of is…
4. When I shut down, what I'm really protecting is…
5. When I demand, what I'm really asking for is…

Then share your answers in a safe environment.

Closing Prayer

Lord, enter our marriage with Your light. Reveal the wounds that have separated us. Give us humility to acknowledge our pain and compassion to understand each other's. Teach us to love without fear, to communicate without attacking, to draw near without running away. Make our marriage a place of healing, not a repetition of trauma. Amen.

CHAPTER 5
WOUNDED LEADERS WHO WOUND

The Danger of Leadership Without Healing**

Leadership is a privilege, but it is also a profound emotional and spiritual responsibility. A leader does not guide only with words, but with the heart. And when that heart is wounded, confused, or hardened, leadership becomes a double-edged sword.

This chapter does not seek to point fingers or condemn wounded leaders. It seeks to understand them, heal them, and restore them—because many of them never had a safe space to be vulnerable. Many learned to lead from survival, not from wholeness.

1. THE LEADER WHO LEARNED TO BE STRONG TOO SOON

Many leaders grew up in environments where they had to mature before their time. They were the responsible ones, the protectors, the problem-solvers, the caretakers, the ones who held everything together.

That "strong" child became an adult who:

- Does not ask for help
- Does not show weakness
- Does not acknowledge exhaustion
- Does not express emotions
- Does not allow others to care for them

Leadership becomes their identity, their refuge, and their armor. But behind that strength lies a tired heart.

2. LEADERSHIP AS A DEFENSE MECHANISM

For many, leading is not only about serving. It is about protecting themselves.

Leadership becomes:

- A way to control what they could not control in childhood
- A way to avoid feeling vulnerable
- A refuge to hide insecurities
- A stage where they can receive validation
- A role that gives them worth when they do not feel it internally

Not all leaders seek power. Many seek safety.

3. THE WOUNDED LEADER WHO HURTS WITHOUT MEANING TO

A wounded leader does not hurt others out of malice. They hurt because they lead from their wound.

Signs of a wounded leader:

- Authoritarianism disguised as firmness
- Excessive control
- Lack of empathy
- Difficulty delegating
- Exaggerated reactions
- Inability to receive correction
- Need for recognition
- Extreme sensitivity to criticism

They are not a bad leader. They are an unhealed leader.

4. THE DANGER OF LEADERSHIP WITHOUT VULNERABILITY

A leader who cannot be vulnerable becomes a leader who is isolated. And an isolated leader is a leader at risk.

Risk of:

- Burnout
- Emotional abuse
- Impulsive decisions
- Broken relationships
- Loss of spiritual sensitivity

- Confusing authority with control
- Confusing obedience with loyalty

Vulnerability does not weaken the leader. It humanizes them.

5. THE IMPACT ON THE CHURCH, THE FAMILY, AND THE COMMUNITY

When a wounded leader leads, their wound filters into everything they touch.

In the church:

- A culture of fear is created
- Respect is confused with submission
- Healthy confrontation is avoided
- Control is spiritualized

In the family:

- Perfection is demanded
- Emotions are minimized
- Provision is confused with connection

In the workplace or community:

- Leadership is driven by pressure
- Empathy is lost
- Tense environments are created

Wounded leadership not only affects the leader, but it also affects everyone who follows them.

6. THE RESTORATION OF THE LEADER: A POSSIBLE PROCESS

A leader's healing begins when they recognize that they are also human. That they also need help. That they also have wounds. That they also deserve rest.

Steps toward restoration:

- Acknowledging the wound
- Seeking emotional or spiritual support
- Practicing vulnerability with safe people
- Delegating without fear
- Learning to receive correction
- Developing empathy
- Connecting with their inner child
- Allowing God to touch protected areas

A healthy leader is not perfect. They are aware.

7. HOW TO SUPPORT A WOUNDED LEADER

Leaders also need care. But they rarely ask for it.

Ways to support them:

- Listen without judgment
- Validate their emotions
- Offer support without invading

- Remind them they are not alone
- Create safe spaces for vulnerability
- Pray for them without pressuring
- Help them rest without guilt

A supported leader is a strengthened leader.

PRACTICAL EXERCISE: "MY LEADERSHIP AND MY WOUND"

Answer honestly:

1. Which part of my leadership comes from my wound?
2. Which part comes from my calling?
3. What do I struggle to delegate, and why?
4. Which emotions do I avoid showing as a leader?
5. What do I need but don't know how to ask for?

Then write this declaration:

"My leadership does not depend on my perfection, but on my healing."

Closing Prayer

> *Lord, heal my heart as a leader. Show me the areas where I have led from my wound. Give me humility to recognize my limits and courage to seek help. Make me a leader who loves, not one who controls. Who guides, not one who dominates. Who serves, not one who hides behind the role. Restore my heart so I may restore others. Amen.*

CHAPTER 6
THE SPIRITUAL COST OF UNHEALED TRAUMA

When the Wound Distorts the Image of God

Trauma affects more than the mind and emotions. It also affects the way we see God. Childhood wounds act as an emotional lens that distorts our spiritual perception. We do not see God as He is... we see Him through the way we learned to see the figures who shaped us.

This is why many people:

- Love God, but cannot trust Him
- Serve God, but cannot rest in Him
- Seek God, but feel He is distant
- Believe in God, but live as if they were alone

It is not a lack of faith. It is not rebellion. It is not spiritual coldness. It is unhealed emotional pain.

Although my father never mistreated me personally—being the youngest—I did not have a positive relationship with him. I grew up hearing the hatred, resentment, and rejection that my family expressed toward him, and those voices shaped my perception. Over time, all of that planted in me a deep resentment, to the point of hating him with all my heart. This affected my relationship with God, even though I didn't know it, until He Himself revealed the root of that pain to me.

My Own Story With This Distortion

In my first book, *Learning To Fly Over The Storm* (2010), I shared how God dealt with me to restore my relationship with Him. I loved God, but my walk was inconsistent. I would draw near, then pull away. I served passionately, then felt empty. I couldn't understand why I couldn't remain firm in my faith.

I didn't know the root was in my wounded heart. I didn't know my soul was still interpreting God through the pain I had experienced with my earthly father. It was in a moment of deep revelation that God showed me something that transformed my life: I could not fully relate to my Heavenly Father while holding resentment toward my earthly father.

Forgiving my father was not justifying what happened. It was not minimizing the pain. It was freeing my heart so I could see God as He truly is—loving, present, safe, constant. That act of forgiveness opened a spiritual door I didn't know was closed. It allowed me to experience God without filters, without fear, without distortion.

In this chapter, we will explore how unhealed trauma affects our spirituality, our identity, our ability to trust God, and the way we interpret His love.

It also reveals how inner healing—this deep work that only God can do—opens the door to a freer, safer, and truer faith. Because when the wound is healed, the image of God becomes clear. And when the image of God becomes clear, the soul finally rests.

1. THE WOUND THAT BECOMES EMOTIONAL THEOLOGY

We all have a biblical theology and an emotional theology. Biblical theology is what we know about God. Emotional theology is what we feel about Him. When there is trauma, these two theologies collide.

- The Bible says: "God is love."
    - The wound says: "Love hurts."
- The Bible says: "God is Father."
    - The wound says: "Fathers abandon."
- The Bible says: "God cares for you."
    - The wound says: "No one cares for me."

The wound becomes the interpreter of faith.

2. THE IMAGE OF GOD SHAPED BY THE IMAGE OF OUR PARENTS

Our relationship with God is often formed through our relationship with parental figures.

- If you had an absent father:
    - You may feel God is distant.
- If you had a cold or a critical mother:
    - You may feel God judges you.
- If you grew up with extreme demands:
    - You may feel God is never satisfied with you.
- If you experienced abuse or violence:
    - You may feel God is unpredictable or severe.
- If you grew up without affection:
    - You may feel God tolerates you, but does not love you.

It is not that God is like that; it is that the wound taught you to see Him that way.

3. SPIRITUALITY AS ESCAPE: WHEN SERVING REPLACES HEALING

Many wounded people hide in spiritual activity to avoid facing their pain.

- They serve so they don't feel.
- They work so they don't think.
- They help, so they don't look inward.
- They stay busy, so they don't confront their story.

Spirituality becomes anesthesia, not healing.

Signs of avoidant spirituality:

- Serving without resting
- Praying without opening the heart
- Helping without allowing oneself to be helped
- Reading the Bible without applying it personally
- Avoiding vulnerability in the church
- Using verses to cover emotions

This is not faith. It is spiritual survival.

4. EMOTIONAL DISCONNECTION AS SPIRITUAL DISCONNECTION

When a person is emotionally disconnected, they also disconnect spiritually. Not because they don't love God, but because they cannot *feel* Him.

Emotional disconnection produces:

- Empty prayers
- Worship without surrender
- Bible reading without revelation
- Service without joy
- Intellectual faith, not relational faith
- Difficulty sensing God's presence

A hardened heart not only blocks emotions. It blocks spiritual experiences.

5. GUILT AND SHAME: ENEMIES OF INTIMACY WITH GOD

Toxic shame makes a person feel unworthy of God's love.

Chronic guilt makes a person live in spiritual debt.

Shame says: "I am not enough for God."
Guilt says: "I don't do enough for God."
Both distort the relationship.

The person lives trying to earn a love they already have. They serve to be accepted instead of serving because they are loved.

6. FAITH AFFECTED BY TRAUMA: COMMON PATTERNS

1. Fear of intimacy with God, because intimacy means vulnerability.
2. Difficulty trusting, because trust was dangerous in childhood.
3. Spiritual perfectionism, the person fears failing.
4. Dependence on leaders, seeking substitute parental figures.
5. Avoiding deep prayer, fearing what God might reveal.
6. Feeling unworthy of God's love, because the wound says, "I have no value."

7. SPIRITUAL HEALING BEGINS WITH EMOTIONAL TRUTH

God does not heal what we pretend. He heals what we acknowledge. Spiritual healing begins when a person can say:

> "Lord, this is my wound. This is how I really see You. This is how I really feel."

Emotional honesty opens the door to spiritual revelation.

8. GOD IS NOT OFFENDED BY YOUR WOUND: DIVINE COMPASSION

God is not scandalized by your trauma.
He is not offended by your fear.
He is not bothered by your distrust.
He does not withdraw because of your confusion.
He knows your story.
He saw your childhood.
He was there when no one else was.
He understands why trust is hard for you.
He knows why you protect yourself.
God does not demand perfection.
God offers presence.

9. RESTORING THE IMAGE OF GOD

Spiritual healing involves replacing the distorted image of God with the true one.

> *God is not distant. He is near.*
> *God is not critical. He is compassionate.*
> *God is not demanding. He is patient.*
> *God is not unpredictable. He is faithful.*
> *God is not violent. He is protective.*
> *God is not indifferent. He is love.*

Emotional healing reveals the true God.

PRACTICAL EXERCISE: IDENTIFYING MY DISTORTED BELIEFS ABOUT GOD

Answer honestly:

1. What do I truly feel when I think about God?
2. What part of my childhood influences that perception?
3. What image of God did I inherit from my parents or caregivers?
4. What do I struggle to believe about God's love?
5. What biblical truth do I need to embrace today?

Then write this declaration:

"Lord, show me who You truly are, beyond my wounds."

. . .

Closing Prayer

Lord, heal my image of You. Free me from the distortions my wound created. Show me Your love as Father, Your compassion as Friend, Your nearness as Healer. Restore my heart so I may see You clearly, trust without fear, and love You without reservation. Amen.

CHAPTER 7

THE ENCOUNTER WITH CHRIST THE HEALER

Jesus and the Brokenhearted

There are wounds no human being can touch. Some pains cannot be explained with words. There are voids no human affection can fill. Some traumas cannot be resolved by therapy, counseling, or willpower alone. There are wounds only Christ can heal.

God gave me a vision that revealed the truth of the human heart—a vision in a dream that marked my spirit. In the dream, I saw a church, and from every direction, people were walking toward it. But they were not coming as we usually imagine them: dressed, smiling, or strong. No. They were coming as if dying.

I saw them dragging themselves with difficulty, as if every step cost them their life. They had open, bleeding wounds. Their faces were marked by sadness, disappointment, and emotional exhaustion. Some looked as if they were about to collapse. Others walked bent under the weight of their pain.

But there was something else—something that shook me.

> They all carried a mask in their hands. A clean, perfect mask, without wounds. A mask that showed no pain, no sadness, no shame. And when they entered the doors of the church... they put it on.

In an instant, their wounded faces disappeared behind a false expression of normalcy. Their tears were hidden. Their wounds were covered. Their pain was silenced.

They entered the house of God... but they did not enter as they truly were.

This is how many arrive at the house of God—wounded, broken, bleeding... but wearing a mask.

> A mask of strength.
> A mask of spirituality.
> A mask of "I'm fine."
> A mask that hides what
> the soul can no longer carry.

Jesus Does Not Touch Masks... Jesus Touches Hearts

In that vision, it became clear that many come to Jesus inside the temple this way. But Jesus did not look at the masks. He did not look at appearances. He did not look at religious posture. Jesus looked at the heart behind the mask—and that is what He showed me. Not what is seen at first glance, but what a wounded heart hides, what a surviving and weary soul conceals to maintain its social standing before others.

But today the Lord says:

"I came for them. For those who cannot go on. For those bleeding on the inside. For those who learned to hide their pain in order to survive."

This chapter is an invitation to encounter Jesus not as a religious figure, not as a concept, not as a tradition... but as the Healer of the soul.

As the One who enters the places no one else can enter.
As the One who touches what no one else can touch.
As the One who restores what seemed lost.
As the One who sees beyond the mask and says to you today:

> "Show me your wound.
> I will not reject you.
> I will not judge you.
> I came to heal you."

Because Jesus is not impressed by the mask. He moves according to the truth of the heart. And when a wounded heart dares to remove the mask before Him... healing begins.

1. Jesus, the One Who Sees What Others Do Not See

In the Gospels, Jesus always drew near to the broken. He

never ignored human pain. He never minimized a wound. He never rejected a shattered heart. He saw:

- The rejected
- The ashamed
- The abandoned
- The abused
- The sick
- The invisible
- The one who cried in silence
- The one carrying guilt that wasn't theirs

Jesus not only sees your wound. He understands it. He knows your entire story—what you lived, what you hid, what you lost, and what marked you. And who better than Him to heal your wounded and mistreated heart.

2. JESUS DOES NOT APPROACH YOUR MASK—HE APPROACHES YOUR TRUTH

Human beings relate through masks. Through roles. Through defenses. Through edited versions of ourselves.

- But Jesus does not relate to your mask.
    - He relates to your truth.
- He does not seek your perfection.
    - He seeks your heart.
- He does not ask you to fix yourself before coming.
    - He asks you to come as you are.
- Because healing does not begin with strength.
    - It begins with honesty.

3. JESUS AND THE BROKEN: A DIVINE PATTERN

Throughout Jesus' earthly ministry, we see something unique and characteristic of Him. Every time Jesus encountered someone wounded, something profound happened.

- With the Samaritan woman, He healed her shame.
- With the Gadarene man, He healed his identity.
- With the woman with the issue of blood, He healed her rejection.
- With Peter, He healed his guilt.
- With Thomas, He healed his doubt.
- With the paralytic, He healed his helplessness.
- With the leper, He healed his loneliness.

Jesus not only heals bodies.
He heals stories.

4. JESUS ENTERS WHERE OTHERS CANNOT ENTER

There are places within you that no one knows.

Places where you stored:

- Fear
- Shame
- Secrets
- Trauma
- Memories

- Silence
- Uncried tears

Jesus enters there. He enters:

- The room where you cried alone
- The moment you were wounded
- The scene that marked you
- The word that destroyed you
- The absence that broke you
- The betrayal that froze you

He does not enter to accuse or judge you. He has entered to restore you. With Him, there is no risk of deception, abandonment, or betrayal. His presence is the safest place for your release, your truth, and your healing. With Jesus, even what seemed irreparable begins to breathe again.

5. THE HUMILITY OF CHRIST: THE ANTIDOTE TO NARCISSISM

Defensive narcissism is born from fear. The humility of Christ is born from love. Jesus did not come to impose Himself. He came to serve. He came to love. He came to heal. His humility is not weakness. It is emotional and spiritual strength. When a wounded person encounters the humility of Christ, something melts inside them.

The mask falls. The defense softens. The heart opens.
The humility of Christ is medicine
for the hardened soul.

6. THE COMPASSION OF CHRIST: BALM FOR SHAME

> Shame says: "I am not enough."
> Jesus says: "You are loved."
> Shame says: "I am a mistake."
> Jesus says: "You are My child."
> Shame says: "God is disappointed in me."
> Jesus says, "I came for you."

The compassion of Christ
not only comfort you.
It dignifies you.

7. THE RESTORATION OF THE HEART: A PROCESS, NOT AN EVENT

The encounter with Christ can be instantaneous, but healing is a process.

> *Jesus not only wants to touch your wound. He wants to walk with you. He not only wants you to touch the hem of His garment— He wants you to sit at His table, remain with Him, enjoy His presence and His intimacy.*

The process includes:

- Acknowledging your pain
- Surrendering your burden
- Allowing Him to show you the truth

- Renouncing the lies you believed
- Receiving His love daily
- Practicing vulnerability with Him
- Letting His Word replace your thoughts
- Allowing His Spirit to transform your reactions

Jesus does not heal you to make you perfect.
He heals you to make you free.

8. THE PRESENCE OF CHRIST IN YOUR STORY

Jesus was there in every moment of your life, even when you didn't feel Him.

He was there:

- When you cried
- When you were abandoned
- When you were rejected
- When you were humiliated
- When you were betrayed
- When you were ignored
- When you were blamed
- When you were broken

He did not cause your pain. But He never left you alone in it. And now He wants to walk with you toward restoration.

PRACTICAL EXERCISE: GUIDED ENCOUNTER WITH CHRIST THE HEALER

- Find a quiet place. Breathe deeply. Close your eyes.
- Imagine Jesus approaching you with tenderness—not with judgment, not with hurry, not with demands.
- Ask Him: **"Lord, what part of my heart do You want to heal today?"**
- Wait in silence. Allow Him to show you a memory, an emotion, a wound, or a truth.
- Then write down what you felt or perceived.

Closing Prayer

Jesus, Healer of my soul, enter the places where no one else could enter. Touch my deepest wounds. Heal my shame, my fear, my pain. Show me Your love, Your compassion, and Your truth. Make me free to live without masks, to love without fear, and to walk with You each day. Amen.

CHAPTER 8
HEALING THE INNER CHILD

Recognize, Name, Validate, Process

Inside every adult lives a child. A child who learned to survive the only way they could. A child who carried more than they were able to hold. A child who adapted in order not to lose love, safety, or belonging. A child who, although the body grew, never received the opportunity to heal. Healing the inner child is not a modern psychological concept. It is a deeply spiritual, emotional, and human process. It is allowing the most vulnerable part of you to be seen, heard, and restored. This chapter guides you step by step through that process: recognizing, naming, validating, and processing the story that remained trapped inside you.

1. WHO IS THE INNER CHILD?

The inner child is the deepest emotional part of your being. It is the living memory of your childhood. It is the voice that learned to stay silent. It is the emotion that learned to hide. It is the need that was never met. The inner child holds:

- Your first wounds
- Your first joys
- Your first fears
- Your first losses
- Your first beliefs about yourself
- Your first interpretations of love

It is not a metaphor. It is an emotional reality.

2. SIGNS THAT YOUR INNER CHILD IS WOUNDED

The inner child manifests in adulthood in subtle but constant ways. Common signs:

- Extreme sensitivity to rejection
- Fear of being alone
- Need for approval
- Difficulty setting boundaries
- Fear of vulnerability
- Exaggerated reactions to criticism
- Perfectionism
- Emotional dependence
- Self-sabotage
- Fear of being seen
- Difficulty trusting

These reactions are not immature; they are activated emotional memories.

3. RECOGNIZE: THE FIRST STEP TOWARD HEALING

You cannot heal what you do not recognize. The first step is to look inward with honesty. Ask yourself:

- What part of me reacts like a child?
- What situations make me feel small, insecure, or afraid?
- Which childhood wounds still hurt when I remember them?

Recognition is not blame. It is illumination.

4. NAME: GIVING LANGUAGE TO WHAT YOU LIVED

The inner child had no words to describe what they lived. Only sensations. That is why naming your experience is an act of liberation.

Examples:

- "I felt alone."
- "I felt ignored."
- "I felt insufficient."
- "I felt responsible for everything."
- "I felt invisible."
- "I felt guilty for things that were not my fault."

Naming transforms chaos into clarity.

5. VALIDATE: GIVING PERMISSION TO YOUR STORY

The inner child does not need correction. They need validation. To validate means to say:

- "What you lived was real."
- "Your pain makes sense."
- "You were not exaggerating."
- "It was not your fault."
- "You deserved love, care, and protection."

Validation breaks shame. Shame heals when exposed to truth.

6. PROCESS: RELEASING WHAT REMAINED TRAPPED

Processing is not reliving the trauma. It is releasing the emotion that remained frozen. Ways to process:

- Crying what you could not cry
- Writing what you could never say
- Talking with someone safe
- Praying from vulnerability
- Allowing Jesus to enter the memory
- Expressing repressed emotions
- Confronting false beliefs
- Replacing lies with truth

Processing allows the trapped emotion to find a way out.

7. DIALOGUE WITH THE INNER CHILD: A POWERFUL TOOL

Talking to your inner child is not a fantasy. It is a deeply transformative, therapeutic, and spiritual practice. It is symbolic, but internally real—helping you confront what you could not face as a child because you did not have the capacity you have today.

Example of dialogue:

- **Adult:** "I know you're scared. I'm not going to ignore you."
- **Inner child:** "Will you leave me as they did before?"
- **Adult:** "No. I'm here. You're not alone."
- **Inner child:** "Can I cry?"
- **Adult:** "Yes. You can cry. I'm with you."

This dialogue repairs what childhood broke.

8. CHRISTIAN REPARENTING: LETTING GOD BE FATHER

Healing the inner child is not only a psychological process. It is a spiritual one. God not only wants to heal your wound. He wants to reparent you—to be the Father you didn't have, the Mother you needed, the safety you lacked, the voice you never heard. He says to you:

- "You are My beloved child."
- "I am with you."

- "I will not leave you."
- "You don't have to be strong all the time."
- "You can rest in Me."

The inner child heals when they find a safe Father.

9. INTEGRATION: WHEN THE INNER CHILD STOPS RUNNING YOUR LIFE

Healing does not mean eliminating the inner child. It means integrating them. When the inner child heals:

- They no longer react with fear
- They no longer demand love
- They no longer hide
- They no longer sabotage relationships
- They no longer seek approval
- They no longer fear being seen

The adult takes the wheel. The inner child rests. In other words, you let go of the child and embrace the new adult in Christ.

PRACTICAL EXERCISE: LETTER TO THE INNER CHILD

Write a letter beginning with:

"Dear child who lives within me, I want to talk to you…"

Include:

- What they lived
- What they felt
- What they needed
- What they deserved
- What you, as an adult, can do now

End with:

"You are no longer in control. I am here to take over for you."

Closing Prayer

> *Lord, take my inner child by the hand. Heal me from the root. Show me the wounds that still hurt and give me courage to face them with Your love. Validate my story, restore my identity, and teach me to live from freedom, not from fear. Amen.*

CHAPTER 9
RELEARNING TO LOVE WITHOUT FEAR

Vulnerability as a Path to Freedom

Loving is a risk. Loving means opening the heart, revealing oneself, giving, trusting, and exposing oneself. That is why those who grew up with childhood trauma often love with fear. Fear of being hurt. Fear of being rejected. Fear of being abandoned. Fear of not being enough. When love was unsafe in childhood, the heart learns to protect itself with walls, masks, and silence. It learns to survive, not to love. But true love cannot flourish where fear rules, because fear shrinks the soul, limits connection, and distorts the way we relate.

Vulnerability, though it may feel dangerous, is the bridge to emotional freedom. It is the space where we stop hiding and begin to be. It is the place where the Holy Spirit invites us to release the defenses that were once necessary but no longer serve us today. Although trauma taught us to protect ourselves, the Holy Spirit teaches us to love. He leads us into a love that is born not from pain but from identity; a love sustained not by fear but by truth; a love that does not depend on the past but on the healing presence of God.

This chapter is a guide to relearning love from healing, not from defense; from freedom, not from fear. Here you will explore how to open your heart without losing yourself, how to love without disappearing, how to trust without silencing your voice, and how to allow God to restore the capacity to love that trauma tried to extinguish. Relearning to love without fear is a process, an act of courage, and a gift of grace. And it begins with one step: daring to be vulnerable before God and, little by little, before those He has placed in your life.

1. LOVE LEARNED THROUGH THE WOUND

Childhood trauma teaches a distorted way of loving. A child does not learn from reality but from the wound; not from love but from pain-shaped perception. Their heart interprets the world through what they lived, not through what they deserved. The wounded child learns that:

- Loving is dangerous
- Depending is risky
- Expressing emotions is shameful
- Trusting is exposing oneself
- Ssking for affection is a weakness
- Showing need is rejection

This learning becomes an emotional pattern carried into adulthood. Without realizing it, the person continues loving from what they lived—loving from survival, not from healing. Thus, the adult unconsciously repeats the emotional logic of childhood. The wounded adult loves:

- With distance
- With control
- With fear
- With demands
- With silence
- With defenses
- With self-sufficiency
- With distrust

Not because they don't want to love, but because they don't know how to love without feeling threatened. Their heart longs for connection, but their story learned protection. And between both worlds, love becomes an internal battlefield.

2. FEAR AS THE ENEMY OF LOVE

Fear is the emotion most incompatible with love.

- Fear says: "Protect yourself."
- Love says: "Give yourself."
- Fear says: "Don't trust."
- Love says: "Open your heart."
- Fear says: "You will be hurt."
- Love says: "It's worth trying."

Fear does not destroy love instantly.

- It erodes it slowly.
- It dims connection
- It blocks intimacy
- It distorts communication
- It creates suspicion
- It generates distance
- It feeds insecurities

Fear is not an external enemy. It is an internal memory.

3. VULNERABILITY: THE BRIDGE TO TRUE LOVE

Vulnerability is the ability to show yourself without masks.

To say: "This is who I am. This is what I feel. This is what I need. This is what I fear."

Vulnerability is not weakness.
It is emotional courage.
Vulnerability allows:
Deep connection, Real intimacy, Mutual trust
Honest communication, Authentic relationships
Without vulnerability, love is superficial.
With vulnerability, love is transformative.

4. EMPATHY: THE LANGUAGE OF A HEALTHY HEART

Empathy is the ability to feel with another person—to step into their world, to listen without judging, to understand without defending yourself.

Empathy is impossible when the heart is in survival mode. But when the heart heals, empathy blossoms. Empathy heals:

- It reduces conflict
- It increases connection
- It strengthens trust
- It softens defenses
- It creates emotional safety

Empathy is the language of mature love.

5. RELEARNING TO LOVE: A GRADUAL PROCESS

Loving without fear is not an event. It is a process.

Stage 1: Recognizing My Defenses

- Do I shut down?
- Do I attack?
- Do I distance myself?
- Do I freeze?

Stage 2: Identifying My Fears

- What do I fear losing?
- What do I fear feeling?
- What do I fear repeating?

Stage 3: Practicing Safe Vulnerability

- Expressing emotions
- Asking for support
- Sharing needs
- Speaking from the heart

Stage 4: Receiving Love Without Suspicion

- Accepting gestures
- believing words
- allowing closeness

Stage 5: Loving From Freedom

- Without controlling
- without demanding
- Without manipulating
- Without fear

Healthy love is built step by step.

6. LOVE AS A DECISION, NOT A REACTION

Mature love does not depend on emotional state.

It is a daily decision. To love is to choose:

- To listen when I want to defend myself
- To draw near when I want to run
- To speak when I want to stay silent
- To forgive when I want to withdraw
- To trust when I want to suspect
- To be vulnerable when I want to protect myself

Love is not automatic. It is intentional.

7. THE HOLY SPIRIT AS TEACHER OF LOVE

The Holy Spirit not only heals wounds. He also teaches us how to love. He produces:

- Patience
- Kindness
- Gentleness
- Self-control
- Compassion
- Humility
- Forgiveness
- Tenderness

Human love is limited. God's love is limitless. And when the Holy Spirit transforms the heart, love flows without fear.

8. LOVING WITHOUT FEAR DOES NOT MEAN LOVING WITHOUT BOUNDARIES

- Loving without fear is not allowing abuse.
- It is not tolerating disrespect.
- It is not accepting mistreatment.
- It is not losing identity.

Loving without fear means:

- Loving from freedom
- Loving the truth
- Loving from healing
- Loving from identity in Christ

Healthy love has boundaries. Boundaries protect love.

PRACTICAL EXERCISE: "WHAT I FEEL, WHAT I NEED, WHAT I ASK FOR"

Complete these sentences:

1. When I shut down, what I really feel is...
2. When I get angry, what I really need is...
3. When I distance myself, what I really fear is...
4. When I demand, what I'm really asking for is...
5. When I love, I want to learn to...

Then share these reflections with someone you trust.

Closing Prayer

> *Lord, teach me to love without fear. Heal my defenses, my fears, and my wounds. Make me brave enough to be vulnerable, humble enough to ask for help, and free enough to love as You love. May Your Holy Spirit transform my heart and teach me to love from truth, not from trauma. Amen.*

CHAPTER 10
RESTORED RELATIONSHIPS

**Healing That Transforms Marriages,
Families and Communities**

Emotional healing is not an isolated process. When a person begins to heal, their relationships also begin to transform. Inner restoration, sooner or later, becomes visible on the outside. It does not happen overnight; it takes time, but the most important thing is taking the first step. As the heart heals, there is no longer a need for masks, because masks are nothing more than defense mechanisms. Psychological literature describes the *"narcissistic mask"* as a structure created to hide deep vulnerability (Back & Morf, 2020). When that vulnerability is acknowledged and restored, the mask loses its function. This chapter explores how personal healing impacts marriage, family, community, and spiritual life. Because when the heart stops reacting from the wound and begins responding from truth, relationships stop being battlefields and become spaces of encounter, connection, and growth.

1. RESTORATION BEGINS WITHIN YOU

Before restoring relationships, God restores your inner world. You cannot give what you do not have. You cannot love from a broken heart. You cannot connect from a disconnected heart. Inner restoration produces:

- Emotional clarity
- Empathy
- Humility
- The ability to ask for forgiveness
- The ability to forgive
- Healthy boundaries
- Honest communication
- Love without fear

Relational restoration is a fruit, not a forced effort.

2. RESTORATION IN MARRIAGE: FROM CONFLICT TO CONNECTION

When one or both spouses begin to heal, the marriage undergoes a profound shift. Emotional dynamics soften, communication becomes more honest, and the atmosphere of the home begins to reflect peace instead of tension.

You may notice visible changes such as:

- Fewer impulsive reactions
- More honest conversations
- Fewer defenses

- More vulnerability
- Fewer accusations
- More empathy
- Less distance
- More connection

Marriage stops being a place where wounds are triggered and becomes a place where wounds are healed.

Keys to marital restoration:

- Speak from the heart, not from the wound
- Listen without interrupting
- Validate emotions
- Apologize without excuses
- Forgive without bringing up the offense
- Create spaces for emotional connection
- Practice safe vulnerability

A restored marriage is not perfect. It is conscious, compassionate, and honest.

It is a space where both partners acknowledge their wounds without using them as weapons.

It is a relationship where vulnerability becomes a bridge, not a threat.

It is a daily commitment to choose love over pride, truth over silence, and connection over fear—transforming future generations in the process.

3. RESTORATION IN THE FAMILY: HEALING GENERATIONS

Unhealed trauma is inherited. But healing is inherited, too. When one person heals, they break generational cycles of:

- Silence
- Emotional abuse
- Abandonment
- Criticism
- Coldness
- Harsh demands
- Shame
- Disconnection

Family restoration includes:

- Conversations that were never had
- Apologies that were never spoken
- Boundaries that never existed
- Hugs that were never given
- Words that were never heard

The family does not always change at the same pace.

But the light that enters through one person illuminates everyone.

4. RESTORATION IN THE COMMUNITY: MORE HUMAN RELATIONSHIPS

When a person heals, their way of relating changes.

Before healing:

- Suspicion
- Defensiveness
- Comparisons
- Competition
- Isolation

After healing:

- Collaboration
- Empathy
- Openness
- Trust
- Connection

The community becomes a safe space, not a place of threat.

5. RESTORATION IN THE CHURCH: FROM RELIGION TO RELATIONSHIP

The church is a place where many wounds are triggered, but also where many are healed. When a person heals emotionally, their spirituality deepens.

Visible spiritual changes:

- Less guilt
- More grace
- Less perfectionism
- More authenticity
- Less religiosity
- More relationship
- Less fear
- More freedom

The church stops being a place where people perform and becomes a place where people *are*.

6. FORGIVENESS: THE KEY TO RESTORATION

Forgiveness is not forgetting. It is not justifying. It is not minimizing. It is not automatic reconciliation. Forgiveness is releasing the heart from the weight that keeps it tied to the past.

Healthy forgiveness involves:

- Acknowledging the wound
- Validating the pain
- Entrusting justice to God
- Releasing the expectation of repair
- Choosing emotional freedom

Forgiveness does not always restore the relationship. But it always restores the heart.

7. BOUNDARIES: THE PROTECTION OF RESTORATION

Restoring does not mean allowing abuse. It does not mean tolerating disrespect. It does not mean returning to toxic dynamics. Boundaries are part of healing. Healthy boundaries include:

- Saying "no" without guilt
- protecting your peace
- Avoiding destructive conversations
- Stepping away from harmful environments
- Not carrying others' responsibilities
- Not allowing emotional manipulation

Boundaries do not destroy relationships. They purify them.

8. RECONCILIATION: WHEN IT IS POSSIBLE AND WHEN IT IS NOT

Reconciliation is beautiful, but not always possible. It depends on two hearts, not one. Reconciliation is possible when:

- There is repentance
- There is change
- There is responsibility
- There is respect
- There are clear boundaries

Reconciliation is NOT advisable when:

- There is abuse
- There is manipulation
- There is violence
- There is denial of harm
- There is no repentance

> *Restoration does not always mean returning.*
> *Sometimes it means releasing.*

Releasing expectations, releasing stories that cannot be repaired, releasing bonds that are no longer healthy. Sometimes true healing comes when we let go of what ties us to pain and allow God to close chapters we do not know how to end.

9. RESTORATION AS TESTIMONY

A restored life is a living message. You do not need to preach to make an impact. Your transformation speaks for you. Your restoration inspires others to:

- Seek help
- Face their story
- Heal their wounds
- Break cycles
- Draw near to God

Personal restoration becomes collective restoration.

PRACTICAL EXERCISE: RELATIONAL RESTORATION PLAN

Write down three relationships you desire to restore. For each one, answer:

1. What wound affects this relationship?
2. What can I do to improve it?
3. What boundaries do I need to establish?
4. What do I need to forgive?
5. What do I need to ask forgiveness for?
6. What can I do this week to take one step toward restoration?

Closing Prayer

Lord, restore my relationships. Heal what was broken, illuminate what became dark, and transform what became hardened. Give me humility to ask for forgiveness, wisdom to set boundaries, and love to build healthy connections. Make my life a testimony of Your restoration. Amen.

CHAPTER 11
A NEW IDENTITY IN CHRIST

From Survivor to Beloved Child

Emotional healing does not end when you recognize your wound... that is only where it begins. It does not end when you understand your story... that is when you begin to understand the purpose behind your existence. It does not end when you embrace your inner child... that is when you finally realize it is time to grow emotionally and leave behind the wounded child who had to survive.

Emotional healing culminates when you discover who you are in Christ—when you understand that you are not the result of what you lived, but the result of what He did for you.

Scripture teaches that in Christ we are new creations, a foundational truth for emotional restoration (Holy Bible, 1960).

- Your identity is not in your trauma.
- Not in your past.
- Not in your defenses.
- Not in your mistakes.
- Not in your masks.
- Not in what was done to you.
- Not in what you lost.

Your identity is in the One who created you, called you, loved you, and restored you. Your true identity is recovered when you finally recognize that without Him you can do nothing—that you need Him to heal, grow, and develop into the full potential God designed for you in His heart before the foundation of the world.

This chapter is an invitation to walk in that new identity—free, secure, and deeply loved. To stop surviving... and begin living.

1. IDENTITY BEFORE CHRIST: SURVIVING, NOT LIVING

Before knowing Christ, identity is shaped by:

- Wounds
- Experiences
- Spoken words
- Trauma
- Rejection
- Abandonment
- Demands

- Shame
- Fear

A person lives from defense, not from truth. From survival, not from fullness.

Trauma-based identity says:

- "I'm not enough."
- "I have no value."
- "I'm alone."
- "I have to be strong."
- "I can't trust."
- "I must protect myself."

But Christ did not come to improve your old identity. He came to give you a new one.

2. IDENTITY IN CHRIST: A GIFT, NOT AN ACHIEVEMENT

Identity in Christ is not earned.

- It is not deserved.
- It is not built.
- It is not negotiated.
- It is received.

In Christ, you are: A Beloved child, accepted, forgiven, chosen, protected, valued, accompanied, restored, & free

Your identity does not depend on your behavior. It depends on His sacrifice. You are not defined by your mistakes, but by the grace that reached you. You are not the result of your failures, but of the finished work of Christ on your behalf. When you understand this, guilt loses its power, and shame stops ruling your story.

3. FROM EMOTIONAL ORPHAN TO BELOVED CHILD

Childhood trauma creates emotional orphans—people who live as if they have no one to turn to, as if everything depends on them, as if no one holds them. But in Christ, you are no longer an orphan.

- The emotional orphan says, "I have to do it alone."
- The beloved child says, "My Father is with me."
- The emotional orphan says, "No one takes care of me."
- The beloved child says, "God is my refuge."
- The emotional orphan says: "I'm not enough."
- The beloved child says: "I am God's masterpiece."

The identity of a child breaks the identity of a survivor.

4. FROM SHAME TO DIGNITY

Toxic shame is one of trauma's deepest wounds. But Christ not only forgives your sin—He restores your dignity. He reminds you that you are not what was done to you, nor what you did.

In His presence, shame loses its voice and truth regains its place.

- Shame says: "I am a mistake."
- Christ says, "You are My perfect creation."
- Shame says: "I have no worth."
- Christ says, "You were bought with a price."
- Shame says: "God is disappointed in me."
- Christ says, "In you I am well pleased."

The cross not only covers your guilt. It covers your shame.

5. FROM MASK TO UNVEILED FACE

Trauma teaches you to wear masks.

Christ teaches you to live with an unveiled face.

- The mask says: "I must pretend."
- Christ says, "You can be authentic."
- The mask says: "I can't show my wounds."
- Christ says, "My wounds heal you."
- The mask says: "I must be strong."
- Christ says, "My power is made perfect in your weakness."

Identity in Christ allows you to be yourself without fear. It frees you from the need to impress, hide, or prove.

When you know who you are in Him, you no longer live to earn approval—you live from the security of being loved. His truth gives you permission to exist with authenticity and walk in freedom. And it is not a freedom for indulgence, but a freedom in Christ—a freedom that transforms, orders, purifies, and guides you to live according to truth.

6. FROM DEFENSE TO FREEDOM

Trauma creates defenses. Christ creates freedom.

Common defenses:

- Control
- Emotional coldness
- Self-sufficiency
- Distance
- Perfectionism
- Silence
- Hardness

These defenses protected you once, but now they limit you. Christ does not ask you to destroy them—He invites you to surrender them. Because where the Spirit of the Lord is, there is freedom.

7. FROM REACTION TO TRANSFORMATION

- The old identity reacts.
    - The new identity responds.
- Reaction is born from fear.
    - Response is born from truth.
- The old identity acts from the wound.

- The new identity acts from the healing Christ produces.

When you live from your new identity, you are no longer a slave to your impulses—you are guided by the Spirit who gives you self-control and peace. You begin to think before acting.

Before:

- You reacted from fear
- From the wound
- From insecurity
- From shame
- From defense

Now:

- You respond from truth
- From peace
- From security
- From love
- From maturity

Identity in Christ transforms the way you live, love, and relate.

It teaches you to see others through grace, not through the wound.

It allows you to build healthier relationships because you no longer seek to fill emptiness—you share fullness.

8. WALKING IN YOUR NEW IDENTITY: PRACTICAL STEPS

1. **Replace lies with truth.** Identify thoughts that do not come from God and replace them with Scripture.
2. **Speak as a child, not as an orphan.** Change your internal language. Replace negative words with faith-filled affirmations based on God's promises.
3. **Practice vulnerability with God.** Pray from the heart, not from religion. Speak to Him as someone you trust completely.
4. **Surround yourself with healthy relationships.** Identity is strengthened in community.
5. **Live from grace, not effort.** Your worth does not depend on performance.
6. **Allow the Holy Spirit to renew your mind.** Transformation begins in thought.

9. IDENTITY DECLARATIONS IN CHRIST

Declare these truths aloud:

- I am God's beloved child.
- I am not my trauma.
- I am not my past.
- I am not my mistakes.
- I am not my defenses.
- I am accepted, forgiven, and restored.
- I am free to love without fear.

THE WOUNDED CHILD AND THE NARCISSISTIC ADULT

- I am valuable, worthy, and complete in Christ.
- My story is being redeemed.
- My identity is secure in Him.

PRACTICAL EXERCISE: "MY NEW NAME"

In the Bible, God changed names to mark new identities.

Write:

1. The name trauma gave you (e.g., "not enough," "invisible," "unloved").
2. The name Christ gives you (e.g., "beloved child," "chosen," "precious," "free").

Then pray:

"Lord, I renounce the old name life gave me, and I embrace the new name You give me."

Closing Prayer

Lord, thank You for giving me a new identity. Thank You for calling me Your child, for loving me unconditionally, and for restoring what trauma tried to destroy. Today I renounce my masks, my fears, and my lies. I embrace the truth of who I am in You. Help me walk each day as Your beloved child—free, secure, and filled with Your Spirit. Amen.

CONCLUSION
THE STORY DOES NOT END AT THE WOUND

You have reached the end of this book... but not the end of your process. This is not a closing. It is a beginning. Emotional healing is not a destination reached in a single leap. It is a path walked day by day, step by step, with patience, with grace, with courage... and with the faithful companionship of the Holy Spirit.

If you have discovered anything in these pages, it is this:

>Your wound does not define your identity.
>Your past does not determine your future.
>Your trauma is not your name.
>Your pain is not your destiny.
>You are more than what you lived.
>You are more than what was done to you.
>You are more than your defenses,
>your reactions, or your fears.
>You are a child. You are loved. You are seen.
>You are restored. You are free.

But read this with an open heart:
The story does not end at the wound.
The story ends in redemption.
And redemption is not a concept.

It is a person. It is Christ entering the places no one else could enter, touching what no one else could touch, healing what seemed impossible to heal.

This is your moment of spiritual climax. This is the point where heaven leans toward your story. Where God takes your trembling hand and says:

"You did not end here. You are just beginning."

This is the moment when your soul, for the first time in a long time, dares to believe that life can be different. That *you* can be different. That your story can have a different ending than the one pain made you believe. This is the moment when the survivor within you begins to transform into a beloved child. When the wounded child stops hiding. When the weary adult stops running. When your spirit finally breathes.

And now... listen to the whisper that changes destinies

- God is writing a new chapter with you.
- One not born from trauma, but from grace.
- One not born from fear, but from love.
- One not born from the wound, but from restoration.
- A chapter where you no longer walk alone.

- A chapter where you no longer survive... you live.
- A chapter where your voice rises again.

Where your heart feels again. Where your soul trusts again. Where your identity is anchored in Christ and not in your past. *This is not the end. This is the rebirth.* And as you close these pages, something within you opens. *A door. A calling. A promise.*

The best part of your story has not yet been written. And God—your Father, your Healer, your Restorer— He is ready to write it with you.
Your story does not end at the wound.
It begins in restoration.

PROPHETIC DECLARATION

In the name of Jesus, I declare over my life that this is the end of my season of surviving and the beginning of my season of living.

I declare that every wound that marked my childhood loses its power over my identity today.

I declare that every word that hurt me, limited me, or defined me has no authority over my destiny.

I declare that every mask I used to protect myself falls now before the presence of God, and that He clothes me with truth, dignity, and purpose.

Today I proclaim that I am not what was done to me, I am not what I lost, I am not what I feared, I am not what I silenced, I am not what others said I was.

I am who God says I am.

I declare that my heart aligns with the voice of the Father, that my soul comes under His truth, and that my spirit awakens to a new identity.

Today I renounce:

- Rejection and loneliness
- Self-criticism and guilt
- The lie of "I am not enough."

And I receive:

- Love and acceptance
- Restoration and freedom
- Identity, purpose, and fullness

I declare that my story does not end at the wound—my story ends in redemption. And that redemption begins today.

I proclaim that God is writing a new chapter with me—one where I walk without fear, love without reservation, live without masks, and move forward without chains.

I declare that my inner child is healed, my adult self is strengthened, and my spirit is affirmed as a beloved child of the Father.

Today I close this book, but I do not close my process.

Today I close these pages, but I open my heart to the ongoing work of the Holy Spirit.

I declare that the best part of my story has not yet been written, and that God—my Father, my Healer, my Restorer—walks with me into what is coming.

- So I believe it.
- So I receive it.
- So I declare it.

In the mighty name of Jesus.

Amen.

PASTORAL BLESSING

May the Lord, your eternal Father, wrap your heart now with His peace. May His presence surround you like a gentle mantle—healing what still hurts, restoring what was broken, awakening what seemed asleep.

I declare over your life that the grace of God covers you, His love sustains you, and His mighty hand guides you.

May the Holy Spirit illuminate every corner of your soul, bringing clarity where there was confusion, truth where there was deception, and freedom where there were chains.

May Jesus, the Healer of the brokenhearted, enter the memories that still weigh on you, the wounds that still bleed, and the silences that still ache—and may His touch transform everything into life, purpose, and redemption.

May the Father remind you each day that you are not alone, not forgotten, not disqualified. You are His beloved child, His delight, His precious creation.

May your identity in Christ be strengthened with power, may your spirit be fortified, may your mind be renewed, and may your heart expand to receive all that He has prepared for you.

May the Lord open paths where you once saw walls, open doors where you once saw rejection, and lead you to places where your soul can flourish without fear.

May the blessing of the Father, the grace of the Son, and the fellowship of the Holy Spirit accompany you today and every day of your life.

And as you close this book, may you not close your process, but step into a new season of healing, freedom, and fullness.

In the mighty name of Jesus.

Amen.

EPILOGUE
THE BEAUTY OF WHAT GOD RESTORES

When God restores, He does not return things to how they were before. He does not patch. He does not repair superficially. He does not rebuild on old ruins. **He makes all things new.** What God makes new is not a copy of the past. It is something stronger, deeper, steadier, more beautiful. Something that does not resemble what you lost, but what He always intended to give you. Your story is not a failure. It is a testimony. It is living evidence that God enters the places no one else could enter, touches what no one else could touch, and heals what seemed impossible to heal. If you are reading these lines, it means you survived what tried to destroy you. It means your soul endured storms others never saw. It means that even with wounds, you kept walking. It means God held you even when you didn't know He was there.

This book is not just the beginning of a more conscious, freer, more authentic life—one more connected to your purpose. It is the beginning of a season where you no longer react from the wound, but from identity. Where you no longer walk from fear, but from truth.

Where you no longer survive... you live.

May your healing inspire others. May your freedom open doors. May your transformation break cycles that once seemed unbreakable. May your story be light for those who still walk in darkness, waiting for a sign, a word, a hug, a hope. Because you were not healed only for yourself. You were healed to become an instrument of healing.

You were restored to restore.
You were lifted to lift others.

And may you always remember this eternal truth:
What God restores, no one can destroy.
What God raises, no one can tear down.
What God marks, no one can erase.
What God begins, He Himself perfects.

Your story continues...
And the best is still waiting to be written.
And remember:
Your story does not end at the wound.
It begins in restoration.

30-DAY EMOTIONAL HEALING PLAN

A Daily Journey of Inner Restoration

30-DAY EMOTIONAL HEALING PLAN

A DAILY JOURNEY TOWARD RESTORATION

Welcome to this 30-Day Emotional Healing Plan that has been designed as an intentional path of inner restoration, guided by the Word of God, conscious reflection, and the healing presence of the Holy Spirit. Each day invites you to pause, breathe, look within, and allow God to illuminate areas of your heart that may have remained hidden, wounded, or silenced for years.

This is not a rushed program, but a journey of depth. Not a checklist, but a spiritual path. Here you will learn to listen to your soul, recognize your emotions, identify patterns, release burdens, and receive the truth God speaks over you.

Each day includes four essential elements that work together to produce transformation:

- **Scripture:** A biblical passage that opens the heart and sets the spiritual focus for the day.
- **Reflection:** A guided thought that helps you connect the Word with your personal story.
- **Practical Action:** A simple yet meaningful step to integrate healing into your daily life.
- **Short Prayer:** A moment of surrender, connection, and dependence on the Lord.

Allow this plan to become a space of encounter with God, with yourself, and with the truth that sets you free. Day by day, step by step, you will see how the Lord restores your heart, renews your mind, and strengthens your identity in Christ.

This is your time.
This is your process.
This is your path toward emotional healing.

A journey of inner restoration guided by the Word, conscious reflection, and the healing presence of God.

MOTIVATIONAL MESSAGE – DAY 1

"Today, your return to yourself begins."

Today marks a before and after in your story—not because everything will change instantly, but because you have chosen to take the first step. And that first step, even if it seems small, is an act of courage, faith, and self-love. Today, you choose to look inward with honesty, without fear of what you may find, trusting that God will walk with you through every discovery.

Perhaps you come with exhaustion, doubts, or wounds you've carried for years. Perhaps you don't know where to begin or fear stirring painful memories. But today, you are not alone. The Lord is close to the brokenhearted, and He Himself sustains you as you begin this journey.

This day is not about solving everything. It is about opening your heart and allowing the light to enter, recognizing that there is an inner child who learned to survive, but who now deserves to heal. Today, you begin to listen to that child, honor them, and place them in the hands of the One who can restore them.

Take a deep breath. Place your hand over your heart. And declare within yourself:

"I am ready to begin. God is with me."

This is your Day 1. Your starting point. Your first step toward the emotional and spiritual freedom God has prepared for you. Welcome to the process. Welcome to your healing.

WEEK 1 – RECOGNIZING THE WOUND

Day 1 — "Lord, show me my story."

Scripture: Psalm 139:23

Reflection: Healing begins when we allow God to illuminate our story without fear.

Action: Write a prayer asking for revelation about your past.

Prayer: "Lord, show me what I need to see."

———

Day 2 — Identify repressed emotions.

Scripture: Proverbs 20:5

Reflection: Hidden emotions continue speaking even when we try to silence them.

Action: Make a list of emotions you avoid feeling.

Prayer: "Give me courage to feel."

———

Day 3 — Write your life timeline.

Scripture: Psalm 90:12

Reflection: Looking back with honesty helps us understand patterns.

Action: Draw a line from childhood to today, marking key events.

Prayer: "Guide me as I review my story."

Day 4 — Recognize your defenses.

Scripture: Ephesians 4:25

Reflection: Defenses once protected us, but now they may limit us.

Action: Identify three defense mechanisms you use.

Prayer: "Help me release what I no longer need."

Day 5 — Name your primary wound.

Scripture: Jeremiah 6:14

Reflection: Naming the wound is an act of spiritual courage.

Action: Write what you believe your root wound is.

Prayer: "Lord, heal my deepest wound."

Day 6 — Practice emotional honesty.

Scripture: Psalm 51:6

Reflection: Inner truth creates space for restoration.

Action: Express a difficult emotion to someone safe or in your journal.

Prayer: "Make me true within."

Day 7 — **Prayer of surrender.**

Scripture: Matthew 11:28

Reflection: Surrender is not giving up—it is resting.

Action: Write what you need to surrender today.

Prayer: "I receive Your rest, Jesus."

WEEK 2 – HEALING THE INNER CHILD

Day 8 — Identify your inner child.

Scripture: Matthew 18:3

Reflection: Within you lives a child still waiting to be seen.

Action: Describe how you imagine your inner child.

Prayer: "Help me meet that child."

Day 9 — Validate their pain.

Scripture: Psalm 34:18

Reflection: Denied pain becomes chains; validated pain transforms.

Action: Write an affirming phrase: "What you lived was real."

Prayer: "Hold my pain, Lord."

Day 10 — Write a letter.

Scripture: Isaiah 41:10

Reflection: Speaking to your inner child builds a bridge of compassion.

Action: Write a letter from your adult self to your child self.

Prayer: "Teach me to love myself."

Day 11 — Identify false beliefs.

Scripture: John 8:32

Reflection: Many beliefs were born from pain, not truth.

Action: Write three limiting beliefs.

Prayer: "Reveal what is not from You."

Day 12 — Replace them with truth.

Scripture: Romans 12:2

Reflection: Renewing the mind is both spiritual and emotional.

Action: Write a biblical truth to replace each lie.

Prayer: "Renew my mind."

Day 13 — Practice self-compassion.

Scripture: Colossians 3:12

Reflection: Compassion toward yourself is part of healing.

Action: Do one act of kindness toward yourself today.

Prayer: "Teach me to treat myself with tenderness."

Day 14 — Inner-embrace prayer.

Scripture: Zephaniah 3:17

Reflection: God sings over you even in your wounds.

Action: Visualize God embracing your inner child.

Prayer: "Hold me, Lord."

WEEK 3 — RESTORING RELATIONSHIPS

Day 15 — **Identify relational patterns.**

Scripture: Proverbs 4:7

Reflection: We cannot change what we do not recognize.

Action: Write repetitive patterns in your relationships.

Prayer: "Give me wisdom to see."

Day 16 — **Practice safe vulnerability.**

Scripture: 2 Timothy 1:7

Reflection: Vulnerability is not weakness; it is guided courage.

Action: Share something authentic with someone trustworthy.

Prayer: "Guide my heart."

Day 17 — **Speak from the heart.**

Scripture: Ephesians 4:15

Reflection: Truth in love transforms connections.

Action: Have an honest conversation with someone.

Prayer: "Place Your words in my mouth."

Day 18 — Ask for forgiveness.

Scripture: Matthew 5:23–24

Reflection: Asking for forgiveness frees the soul.

Action: Identify someone you need to ask forgiveness from.

Prayer: "Humble my heart with love."

Day 19 — Forgive.

Scripture: Mark 11:25

Reflection: Forgiveness does not excuse, but it liberates.

Action: Write the name of someone you need to forgive.

Prayer: "Help me release."

Day 20 — Set boundaries.

Scripture: Proverbs 4:23

Reflection: Boundaries are acts of self-love and clarity.

Action: Define one boundary you need to implement.

Prayer: "Protect me as I learn."

Day 21 — Prayer for relationships.

Scripture: Romans 12:18

Reflection: Peace is a path we build.

Action: Pray for three important relationships.

Prayer: "Make me an instrument of peace."

WEEK 4 – NEW IDENTITY IN CHRIST

Day 22 — Declare who you are in Christ.

Scripture: 2 Corinthians 5:17

Reflection: Your identity is not in your wound but in your Redeemer.

Action: Write five identity declarations in Christ.

Prayer: "Remind me who I am."

Day 23 — Renounce your old identity.

Scripture: Ephesians 4:22–24

Reflection: Healing requires leaving behind what no longer defines you.

Action: Write what you will no longer accept as identity.

Prayer: "Clothe me with the new."

Day 24 — Receive God's love.

Scripture: Romans 8:38–39

Reflection: God's love is the foundation of all restoration.

Action: Meditate 10 minutes on God's unconditional love.

Prayer: "I open my heart to Your love."

Day 25 — Practice gratitude.

Scripture: 1 Thessalonians 5:18

Reflection: Gratitude shifts perspective and heals the soul.

Action: Write 10 things you are grateful for today.

Prayer: "Thank You for Your faithfulness."

Day 26 — Speak as a child, not an orphan.

Scripture: Romans 8:15

Reflection: Language reveals identity.

Action: Replace one fear-based phrase with one of trust.

Prayer: "Father, teach me to speak as Your child."

Day 27 — Act from freedom.

Scripture: Galatians 5:1

Reflection: Freedom is practiced, not just proclaimed.

Action: Do one action that reflects your freedom in Christ.

Prayer: "I want to walk free."

Day 28 — Identity prayer.

Scripture: 1 Peter 2:9

Reflection: You are chosen, loved, and set apart.

Action: Declare your identity in Christ out loud.

Prayer: "I affirm who I am in You."

Day 29 — Write your testimony.

Scripture: Revelation 12:11

Reflection: Your story has the power to set others free.

Action: Write your healing journey up to today.

Prayer: "Use my story for Your glory."

Day 30 — Celebrate your process.

Scripture: Philippians 1:6

Reflection: God began the work, and He will complete it.

Action: Celebrate your progress with a symbolic act.

Prayer: "Thank You for what You have done in me."

STUDY GUIDE

FOR GROUPS AND LEADERS

12
Sessions
One Per-Chapter

STUDY GUIDE FOR GROUPS AND LEADERS

12 SESSIONS — ONE PER CHAPTER

Introduction to the Study Guide for Groups and Leaders

The Study Guide for Groups and Leaders that accompanies this book was created to facilitate a deep process of emotional healing, spiritual restoration, and personal transformation in a safe, guided, and communal environment. Each session is designed to help participants explore their story, understand their emotional patterns, identify their defenses, and open space for Christ to heal the most vulnerable areas of the heart.

This material can be used by small-group leaders, pastors, counselors, facilitators, married couples, ministry teams, or anyone who desires to walk with others on a journey of growth. It does not require professional counseling training—only a willing heart to listen, accompany, and create an atmosphere of respect, confidentiality, and compassion.

Each session includes five essential elements that work together to create a holistic process:

1. **Objective:** Defines the central intention of the session and guides the conversation toward a clear purpose.
2. **Suggested Scripture Reading:** A carefully selected biblical passage that illuminates the theme from God's perspective and opens the heart to healing truth.
3. **Reflection Questions:** Invite introspection, honesty, and connection with one's emotional story. These questions do not seek "correct" answers, but authenticity.
4. **Practical Activity:** Helps bring the content of the session into personal experience. These are simple yet profound exercises that facilitate emotional understanding, internal expression, and spiritual integration.
5. **Closing Prayer:** Ends each gathering by inviting the Holy Spirit to seal what was learned, bring revelation, and continue the healing work beyond the group.

This guide is designed to move progressively—from recognizing the wound, to understanding defenses, identifying patterns, healing the image of God, encountering

Christ in one's story, restoring relationships, and finally affirming a new identity in Him. Each session builds upon the previous one, allowing the process to be safe, gradual, and transformative.

My prayer is that this guide becomes an instrument of restoration for your life, your family, your church, and your community. May each gathering be a space where truth sets free, love restores, and Christ heals what once seemed impossible.

NOTE TO LEADERS

Dear leader,

Thank you for accepting the call to accompany others in a process as sacred as emotional and spiritual healing. Guiding a group that works through trauma, identity, and restoration requires sensitivity, patience, and a heart willing to listen more than it speaks. You are not here to "fix" anyone, but to create a safe space where the Holy Spirit can work.

Your role is to facilitate, not pressure; to accompany, not direct anyone's life; to hold the space, not carry the stories. Trust that God will do what you cannot do. Your presence, compassion, and willingness are already part of the healing others need.

Remember:

- You are not a therapist—you are a companion.
- You don't need all the answers—only a willing heart.
- You are not alone—the Holy Spirit is the true Counselor.

Thank you for serving with love, humility, and courage.

2. How to Facilitate an Emotional Healing Group

Facilitating a group requires structure, clarity, and a safe environment. Here are essential principles:

1. Establish a Safe Environment

- Absolute confidentiality.
- Respect for each participant's time and voice.
- No one is required to share more than they wish.

2. Be a Guide, Not the Protagonist

- Ask open-ended questions.
- Avoid preaching or correcting testimonies.
- Allow silence—sometimes silence *is* part of healing.

3. **Maintain the Rhythm:** Each session has a purpose. Move forward without rushing, but with direction. If a topic becomes intense, pray, breathe, and continue when the group is ready.

4. **Do Not Force Processes:** Everyone heals at their own pace. Some will cry, others will stay quiet, others will write. All responses are valid.

5. **Pray Before and After:** Ask for discernment, sensitivity, and wisdom. This work is not done in human strength.

6. **Know Your Limits:** If someone needs professional help, recommend it with love. Being a leader does not mean carrying everything.

7. **Celebrate Every Step:** A small emotional step can be a great spiritual miracle.

General Opening Prayer for the Guide

Lord Jesus,

We open this space with hearts willing to listen, learn, and heal. We invite You to walk with us in every session, every conversation, and every memory that comes to light. May Your perfect love cast out all fear, and may Your presence bring peace where there was pain, clarity where there was confusion, and hope where there was silence.

Holy Spirit, guide our words, emotions, and thoughts. Make this group a safe refuge where each person can be seen, heard, and loved. Heal what is broken, restore what was lost, and reveal the truth that sets us free.

Father, we affirm that this process belongs to You. May Your light illuminate every story, and may Your grace sustain every step. We declare that this will be a time of transformation, identity, and deep restoration.

Amen.

WELCOME MESSAGE FOR PARTICIPANTS

Welcome to this journey of healing, truth, and restoration.

This group is not a place for judgment, competition, or appearances. It is a safe space where every story has value, every emotion has a place, and every person is received with dignity and love.

Here, we do not come to prove strength, but to allow God to strengthen us.

We do not come to hide, but to be seen.

We do not come to run, but to walk together.

Throughout these sessions, we will explore wounds, patterns, defenses, and deep truths that have shaped our lives. There will be moments of clarity, moments of confrontation, and moments of comfort. All of it is part of the process.

You are not alone.
You are not broken.
You are not behind.

You are exactly where God wants to begin His work.

Open your heart, be honest with yourself, and allow the Holy Spirit to walk with you step by step. This is a journey toward freedom, identity, and true love.

Thank you for daring to begin.

SESSION 1 – THE CHILD WHO LEARNED TO SURVIVE

Objective: Recognize the emotional root of the wound.

Suggested Scripture: Psalm 34:18

Reflection Questions:

- What did I learn to do in order to survive
- What emotions did I stop feeling

Activity: Emotional timeline.

Closing Prayer:

> Lord, thank You for showing me where my wound began. I give You the child I was and the emotions I learned to hide. Walk with me as I discover what still needs healing. Amen.

SESSION 2 – WHEN THE HEART HARDENS

Objective: Identify emotional defenses.

Suggested Scripture: Ezekiel 36:26

Reflection Questions:

- How do I protect myself
- What is difficult for me to feel

Activity: Emotional journal.

Closing Prayer:

> *Father, show me the defenses I built to survive. Remove my heart of stone and give me a heart that is sensitive, healthy, and free. Amen.*

SESSION 3 – NARCISSISM AS A DEFENSE

Objective: Understand the emotional mask.

Suggested Scripture: 1 Samuel 16:7

Reflection Questions:

- What mask do I wear
- What do I fear showing

Activity: Write "my false self."

Closing Prayer:

> Jesus, reveal the masks I use to protect myself. Teach me to live from truth and not from fear. Look at my heart and transform it. Amen.

SESSION 4 – THE ADULT WHO DEMANDS WHAT THEY NEVER RECEIVED

Objective: Identify unexpressed needs.

Suggested Scripture: James 4:1–3

Reflection Questions:

- What do I expect others to guess

Activity: "What I feel vs. what I say."

Closing Prayer:

> Lord, show me my unexpressed needs and teach me to communicate them with love. Free me from hidden expectations and give me emotional maturity. Amen.

SESSION 5 – MARRIAGES AFFECTED BY TRAUMA

Objective: Recognize relational patterns.

Suggested Scripture: Ephesians 4:31–32

Reflection Questions:

- What triggers my wound in the relationship

Activity: Guided conversation.

Closing Prayer:

God, heal my relational patterns. Help me love with patience, humility, and truth. Restore what trauma damaged. Amen.

SESSION 6 – WOUNDED LEADERS WHO WOUND

Objective: Heal leadership.

Suggested Scripture: John 13:3–5

Reflection Questions:

- What part of my leadership comes from my wound

Activity: Self-evaluation.

Closing Prayer:

Father, purify my leadership. Heal the areas where I have led from my wound and teach me to serve like Jesus—with humility, love, and truth. Amen.

SESSION 7 – THE SPIRITUAL COST OF TRAUMA

Objective: Heal the image of God.

Suggested Scripture: Psalm 27:10

Reflection Questions:

- How do I truly see God

Activity: Replace lies with truth.

Closing Prayer:

> Lord, restore my image of You. Replace the lies I believed with the truth of Your love. Remind me that You have never abandoned me. Amen.

SESSION 8 — THE ENCOUNTER WITH CHRIST THE HEALER

Objective: Invite Jesus into the wound.

Suggested Scripture: Luke 4:18

Reflection Questions:

- What do I know about Christ
- What do I think about healing

Activity: Guided encounter prayer.

Closing Prayer:

> Jesus, enter my deepest wounds. Touch them with Your love and restore what I thought would never heal. I open my heart to You. Amen.

SESSION 9 – HEALING THE INNER CHILD

Objective: Validate the emotional story.

Suggested Scripture: Matthew 18:3

Reflection Questions:

- Have I allowed my inner child to run my life
- Do I justify my behavior with my "wounded child"

Activity: Letter to the inner child.

Closing Prayer:

Father, I embrace the child I once was and place them in Your hands. Heal their pain, restore their voice, and teach me to live from maturity and not from the wound. Amen.

SESSION 10 – RELEARNING TO LOVE WITHOUT FEAR

Objective: Practice vulnerability.

Suggested Scripture: 1 John 4:18

Reflection Questions:

- Do I always want things my way
- Do I expect everyone to give me what I ask

Activity: "What I feel, what I need, what I ask."

Closing Prayer:

> *Lord, teach me to love without fear. Remove my need to control and give me the courage to be vulnerable. Amen.*

SESSION 11 – RESTORED RELATIONSHIPS

Objective: Create a restoration plan.

Suggested Scripture: Colossians 3:12–14

Reflection Questions:

- Do I recognize when I am wrong
- Have I learned to say "I'm sorry"

Activity: Relational plan.

Closing Prayer:

> *God, give me humility to acknowledge my mistakes and courage to ask for forgiveness. Guide me on the path of reconciliation and restoration. Amen.*

SESSION 12 – A NEW IDENTITY IN CHRIST

Objective: Affirm the new identity.

Suggested Scripture: 2 Corinthians 5:17

Reflection Questions:

- Do I recognize who I am in Christ
- Do I struggle to see myself as He sees me

Activity: Identity declarations.

Closing Prayer:

Jesus, I affirm my identity in You. I declare that I am new, free, and loved. Help me walk each day in the truth of who I am in Christ. Amen.

General Closing Prayer for the Program

Beloved Lord,

Today, we close this process with gratitude in our hearts. Thank You for every session, every conversation, every tear, every revelation, and every courageous step taken along the way. Thank You for showing us that we are not defined by our wounds, but by Your love; that we are not the pain we lived, but the work You are forming within us.

Father, we give You everything that came to light—memories, fears, defenses, masks, wounds, and silences. We ask You to continue the work You began, to keep healing what still hurts, restoring what seemed lost, and affirming our identity in Christ.

Holy Spirit, remain with each participant. Be our guide, comfort, truth, and strength. May what we learned here not remain on these pages, but become daily transformation, new decisions, healed relationships, and a life lived in freedom.

Jesus, thank You for walking with us, entering our wounds, and showing us that Your love is stronger than any story. We declare that this process does not end here—it is only beginning.

Amen.

Final Blessing Prayer

> May the Lord bless you and keep you.
>
> May He illuminate your heart with His truth and fill you with peace.
>
> May He heal the memories that still hurt and strengthen the areas where you felt weak.
>
> May He remind you each day that you are loved, seen, and known by Him.
>
> May the Holy Spirit accompany you in every step, guiding you toward healthier relationships, wiser decisions, and a stronger identity in Christ.
>
> May your inner child find rest, your adult self find direction, and your spirit find purpose.
>
> May Jesus be your refuge, your healer, and your truth.
>
> May His perfect love cast out all fear and teach you to love without fear, live without masks, and walk without shame.
>
> And may the work God began in you, He Himself bring to completion.
>
> In the name of the Father, the Son, and the Holy Spirit.
>
> Amen.
>
> Final note to the Reader:

If you would like to share your experience as a reader of *The Wounded Child and the Narcissistic Adult*, or as a leader, pastor, or student who has used this material, it would be an honor to hear from you.

You may write to us at: **jdncpublications@gmail.com or visit us at www.jdnpublications.com or www.jdncorporation.com**

ABOUT THE AUTHOR
GET TO KNOW EDNA L. ISAAC

Edna L. Isaac was born in Aguadilla, Puerto Rico, and moved to the United States at the age of sixteen, where she established her life and ministry in Massachusetts. She has been married to Pastor Francisco J. Isaac for 34 years, and together they have four children. Edna is widely recognized as a professional change agent, author, educator, and international speaker whose work has impacted individuals, churches, and communities across the world.

She is the CEO and President of **JDN Corporation** and **JDN Publications / EDUCATE Publishing**, organizations dedicated to developing resources that uplift, restore, and empower. She is also the co-founder and associate pastor of **Casa de Adoración (CDA House of Worship)** in Taunton, MA, where she serves alongside her husband.

Edna is the founder of several ministries and initiatives, including **Radio WHUC 95.6 FM** (currently under construction), **Entre Amigas Internacional**, the **Association** of Christian Churches and Ministries Inc., and the JDN Global Leadership Network. Her leadership extends beyond the church, having served for almost seven years as president of the Taunton Clergy Association and teaching for more than a decade in two theological institutions: ETME in Boston, MA, and the Getsemaní Bible Institute in New Bedford, MA.

She currently works as a **Senior Counselor** at one of the Community Justice Support Centers in Massachusetts, where they supports individuals navigating emotional, relational, and personal challenges. With more than fourteen published books and contributions as a co-author in multiple projects, Edna has become an influential voice in emotional healing, spiritual identity, and personal growth. Her 2025 publication, *Entre Amigas: Historias del Alma que Inspiran e Impactan*, highlights transformative stories that celebrate the strength and resilience of women.

Her work uniquely blends editorial excellence, educational formation, emotional intelligence, narrative creativity, and pastoral ministry. As a spiritual leader, she has walked with hundreds of individuals through processes of inner restoration, identity formation, and spiritual transformation, becoming a trusted guide for those seeking healing and purpose.

Edna is also a curriculum designer and developer of emotional-growth programs for communities, with a special focus on vulnerable and multicultural populations. Her vision is clear: to equip new generations with tools that transform not only behavior, but the heart.

She is the author of *Learning to Fly Over The Storm* (2010), where she shares her own healing journey and the revelation that restored her identity as a daughter of the Heavenly Father. Her testimony of forgiveness and redemption has become a foundational pillar of her message.

In *The Wounded Child and the Narcissistic Adult*, Edna brings together her pastoral experience, educational background, and deep understanding of emotional trauma to guide readers toward clarity, healing, and spiritual identity. Her writing is warm, honest, and profoundly human—inviting every reader into a journey of self-discovery, freedom, and redemption.

Edna resides in Taunton, Massachusetts, where she continues developing editorial projects, teaching workshops, training leaders, and serving local and international communities with a message of hope, identity, and transformation.

For more information, visit **www.jdnpublications.com**, **www.jdncorporation.com**, or contact **jdncpublications@gmail.com**.

REFERENCES

Back, M. D., & Morf, C. C. (2020). *Narcissism*. In *Encyclopedia of Personality and Individual Differences*. Springer.

EBSCO Research Starters. (n.d.). *Narcissism (psychology)*.

Isaac, E. L. (2010). *Aprendiendo a volar sobre la tormenta*. Xulon Press.

Orth, U., Krauss, S., & Back, M. D. (2024). Development of narcissism across the life span: A meta-analytic review of longitudinal studies. *Psychological Bulletin*.

Santa Biblia. (1960). *Reina-Valera 1960*. Sociedades Bíblicas Unidas.

Wikipedia. (n.d.). *Narcissism*. https://en.wikipedia.org/wiki/Narcissism

Yakeley, J. (2018). Current understanding of narcissism and narcissistic personality disorder. *BJPsych Advances*.

www.ingramcontent.com/pod-product-compliance
Lightning Source LLC
Chambersburg PA
CBHW061759070526
44586CB00023B/2636